Speak Security with a Business Accent

How to communicate cybersecurity concepts clearly, ease friction with stakeholders, and influence decisions

Joshua C Mason

Dedication

I would like to thank my daughters, Annabel and Olivia, for always bringing joy to my day and inspiring me to write something that they might be interested in reading.

To my wonderful wife, Cherie-Lee, who challenges me to always improve and be the best I can be through her example of strength and endurance. Your support and love mean everything to me.

To my friends and mentors along the way who have pushed me to share through talks, podcasts, conferences, and books. I am so glad to have you all around me and to build this community. The list would be so incredibly long, and the people I might forget would make me feel so bad. For that reason, you know who you are, and if you think I'm talking about you, I am. I am.

To the cybersecurity professionals out there trying to make the world safer from criminals and those who would steal, cheat, and scam if we weren't there to do our jobs. Thank you. I hope you find this book helpful and valuable.

Table of Contents

The Flight Line
and the Front Office

I didn't think my career in cybersecurity would start with a commander telling me I wasn't cut out for it.

After nearly a decade in the Air Force flying C-130 tactical airlift and a stint learning to fly drones, my flying career came to an end. The Air Force trained me up and sent me to be a flight commander at the 1st Special Operations Communications Squadron, in the middle of the Air Force's most demanding mission sets: Special Operations. For six months, I fought to keep things running. Not just systems, but priorities, people, and sanity. We were trapped in what I now understand were the Four Types of Work: planned projects, internal maintenance, changes from above, and everyone's favorite, unplanned work that landed in your lap at 4:59 p.m.

Our squadron's mission didn't always align with the needs of the operations squadrons we supported, the wing commander, or anyone who didn't wear our patch. And it showed. Everything felt like a struggle. Meetings went in circles. The outcomes were fuzzy. People burned out.

After six months of trying to align tactical tasks with disconnected strategic goals, my commander pulled me aside and said, "I don't see you having a future in cybersecurity." And just like that, I was reassigned to teach at the Air Force Special Operations School. Finally, back to the pilot world.

At the time, it felt like a relief. No more staff meetings, no more uphill battles over who owned what. But it also planted a seed. Teaching gave me space to think, to lead, and eventually, to influence.

That seed grew slowly through years of training, consulting, and working with pentesters, red teams, blue teams, and everyone in between. I started to notice a pattern: the technical folks were getting better and better at tech, but somehow still losing ground with the business.

We weren't speaking the same language.

Then I read The Phoenix Project, The Goal, and The Unicorn Project. Finally, things clicked. I understood the four types of work. I saw the constraints, the flow, and the leadership challenges, but even in those books, cybersecurity felt like an afterthought.

John, the CISO in The Phoenix Project, eventually figures it out. But his journey is still framed around IT and DevOps. I didn't see a roadmap for the kind of cybersecurity professionals I knew, like me, who try to make security work for the business instead of just working against it.

So, I started giving talks. I told security teams that if they wanted to be heard, they had to speak business.

You don't speak French in Afghanistan. You speak Pashtu. You don't speak Spanish in Berlin. You speak German. And in business? You talk about risk, growth, opportunity, and trust.

I've earned an MBA and hold a CISSP certification. I've been a pilot, pentester, teacher, and strategist. At this point, I feel bilingual and fluent in both tech and business. Yet, even now, I meet security professionals who ask, "Okay, I get it... But what do I do next?"

This book is my answer.

It is not a theory or a script, but a path based on experience, mistakes, coaching, and thousands of conversations.

The work starts here: with how we think, how we speak, and how we choose to lead.

I hope it helps.

Chapter 1:

Introduction

Red warning lights pulsed across the monitors as Maya Tran stood at the threshold of TechForward's security operations center. Three hours into what should have been a routine Friday, chaos had erupted instead. She watched her team, all competent professionals with certifications longer than their surnames, scramble like they'd never seen an incident before.

"I've run every detection rule in our playbook. Nothing's triggering right." Amit's fingers flew across his keyboard, the glow of his screen reflecting off his glasses. "The EDR says we're clean, but the network logs show data leaving through encrypted channels we can't identify."

"That's impossible. We spent six months implementing that zero-trust architecture." Dani slammed her coffee mug down, liquid sloshing onto post-its filled with hastily scrawled IP addresses. "The board approved three million for this security stack. It was supposed to catch exactly this kind of thing."

Maya observed the digital carnage without saying a word. Dashboards designed to provide clarity now obscure it. Alerts meant to prioritize threats are now buried by them. The expensive tools they'd fought to acquire, the ones with all the right analyst ratings and compliance checkboxes, sat useless against whatever was happening.

"Try rolling back to the snapshot from this morning," called out Jerome from the far corner, his voice tight with frustration. "Maybe we can isolate which system was compromised first."

"Already tried. Backup verification is failing. Whatever this is, it knew exactly where to hit us." Amit pushed back from his workstation, running both hands through his hair. "I don't understand. We followed every best practice in the industry."

The room fell into a tense silence broken only by keyboard clicks and the low hum of overworked servers. Maya stepped forward, her mind already assembling patterns from fragments. The problem wasn't with their technology. It was in how they thought about defense, how the entire industry thought about it. Their attacker wasn't following a script, so their defenses couldn't either.

* * *

Maya leaned against the doorframe, letting the crisis wash over her without drowning in it. This wasn't their first incident, and it wouldn't be their last. What troubled her wasn't the breach itself, but the pattern it represented: the growing disconnect between security investment and security outcomes.

Last quarter, she'd presented sobering numbers to the board: the average cost of a data breach had climbed to $4.35 million, with response times averaging 287 days from infiltration to containment. TechForward had poured 12% of their IT budget into security, above industry average, yet here they were, joining the 68% of organizations that'd experienced a successful attack despite increased spending. The math didn't add up, and Maya knew why. They'd built a security program optimized for compliance checkboxes rather than adaptive defense.

She pulled out her phone and scrolled through her notes from last month's CISO summit. The statistics had been grim then, too. Enterprises were spending record amounts on cybersecurity, projected to exceed $170 billion globally this year, yet breaches were increasing, not decreasing. More damning was the data on detection: 60% of successful breaches were still discovered by third parties, not by the expensive tools companies had implemented. And for all the talk about automation and AI-powered responses, human analysts still spent an average of 3.5 hours investigating each legitimate alert.

The industry had a measurement problem. They tracked spending, tool deployment, and compliance coverage, metrics that made for good board presentations but poor security outcomes. What they didn't measure was adaptability, decision speed, or how well teams could synthesize partial information under pressure. The things that actually mattered.

"I need everyone to stop what they're doing," Maya said, her quiet voice somehow cutting through the chaos. The team turned toward her, surprise evident on their tired faces. She rarely intervened directly during incidents, preferring to let her leaders handle the tactical response. But this wasn't a tactical problem.

"We've been playing the game wrong," she continued, stepping fully into the room. "And our opponent knows it."

* * *

This book isn't about adding another security tool or implementing another framework. The cybersecurity industry has been trapped in a cycle of diminishing returns for years: increased spending, greater complexity, heightened burnout, and, paradoxically, more breaches. Most security books offer technical solutions to what is fundamentally a human problem. They prescribe tools instead of mindsets, compliance instead of adaptability, and rigid processes instead of resilient teams.

What if we stopped treating security as a technical discipline and started seeing it as a human one? What if the answer isn't more alerts, more dashboards, and more sleepless nights, but rather better questions, clearer communication, and teams that could bend without breaking? This book won't give you another checklist or promise silver-bullet solutions. Instead, it offers something more valuable: a way to build security that works with human nature rather than against it.

You'll find practical approaches to transform how your organization thinks about risk, responds to threats, and builds lasting resilience. We'll explore how successful security leaders create environments where good security decisions happen naturally, not because of fear or policy, but because they've aligned security with how people actually work and think. Through engaging stories, research-backed insights, and frameworks you can implement immediately, you'll discover why the most secure organizations don't just invest differently, they think differently.

* * *

Maya returned to her desk and opened her notebook. She'd seen this story play out countless times across the industry, different companies, same fundamental challenges. She thought about the SOC analyst at MidCorp she knew, bleary-eyed at 3 AM, drowning in alerts while trying to determine which of the hundreds deserved escalation. The young woman had built an impressive Python script to help triage, but the organization's rigid processes meant she couldn't implement it without months of approval.

Then there was James, the CISO at that healthcare startup. Harvard MBA, technical background, impressive resume, yet Maya had watched him falter in the boardroom when translating technical threats into business risks. He had all the right data but couldn't bridge the gap between security metrics and what the board actually cared about: patient trust, regulatory exposure, and competitive advantage. His team had the tools but lacked the narrative.

She thought of the DevOps engineer who had reached out to her through her gh05t5c1pt handle last week, frustrated that security was seen as the department of "no" rather than an enabler of innovation. He wanted to build security into the pipeline, but couldn't get alignment between teams that spoke different languages, and risk scores meant nothing to developers racing toward deployment deadlines.

And finally, Maya considered the security architect at the financial services firm, who was brilliant at designing controls but struggled with the human element. The perfect security architecture on paper had crumbled when faced with shadow IT, convenience-seeking executives, and third-party integrations that no one had accounted for. All the compliance checkboxes were ticked, but the system wasn't actually secure against how people really behaved.

* * *

This book isn't just for CISOs or technical specialists. It is for anyone caught in the gap between security theory and human reality, the analyst trying to make sense of too much data, the leader translating security into business value, the engineer attempting to build security that enables rather than blocks, and the architect designing for humans rather than hypothetical threats. It is for everyone who has sensed that the conventional approach to security isn't working but can't quite articulate why or how to fix it.

* * *

Maya rubbed her eyes and looked out the window. The security industry has been caught in the same trap for decades: treating influence as a byproduct of technical expertise rather than a discipline in its own right. The Gray Hat's words echoed in her mind: "You're not just here to stop breaches. You're here to build belief."

She thought about what truly made security professionals effective. It wasn't their technical knowledge alone; it was their ability to translate that knowledge into language that resonated with others. It was their capacity to build trust, foster collaboration, and navigate organizational complexities. Above all, it was their ability to make security relevant to the business goals that mattered most.

Maya envisioned security influence as a bridge, not a wall. On one side stood technical expertise: vulnerabilities, controls, and frameworks. On the other side stood business outcomes: revenue protection, customer trust, competitive advantage, operational resilience. Most security professionals spent their careers perfecting one side of the bridge while neglecting the other. They mastered the technical elements but failed to connect them to what the business cared about. They spoke in CVEs (Common Vulnerabilities and Exposures) when executives needed to hear about EBITDA (Earnings Before Interest, Taxes, Depreciation, and Amortization).

These concepts aren't about abandoning technical rigor; it's about amplifying their impact through strategic communication and relationship building. It rests on three pillars: Translation, Trust, and Transformation. Translation means converting security concepts into a language that reflects business value. Trust is built by consistently delivering results and showing genuine empathy. Transformation means changing how security is

11

perceived, from a cost center to a business enabler, from a department of "no" to a catalyst for "yes, safe and effective the first time."

In the boardroom, security isn't measured in patching percentages or vulnerability counts; it is measured in dollars, in risk to revenue, in customer trust preserved or lost. When she'd first started as a CISO, Maya had presented detailed technical metrics that executives politely nodded at but never truly engaged with. The Gray Hat had taught her to speak the language of the boardroom: "If you can't explain security's impact on earnings, you're not in the business conversation."

This approach isn't about manipulation or politics; it is about effectiveness. The most technically correct security program in the world would fail if people didn't understand it, believe in it, or follow it. Security wasn't just a technical challenge; it is a human one. And humans respond to stories, relationships, and relevance more powerfully than they do to policies, controls, or compliance mandates.

* * *

This book is not designed to languish on a shelf or serve as mere theoretical musings. It is a practical manual, forged from real experiences, both triumphs and setbacks. Each chapter is crafted with stories and principles designed for immediate application, not just reflection.

Approach this book with a pen in hand. Highlight the sections that resonate with your current dilemmas. When you stumble upon a principle that aligns with your circumstances, put it into action within the week. Don't wait for ideal conditions; your influence skills will flourish through practice, not perfection.

What sets this book apart is its commitment to practical implementation over academic abstraction. Each chapter will present clear examples of successes and failures, illustrating how security professionals enhanced their efficacy through simple shifts in communication and relationship management. You will discover specific phrases to employ, questions to pose, and strategies to adopt, approaches they can immediately use in their next meeting, email, or presentation. The takeaways will not be theoretical, but actionable insights: methods to translate technical risk into business significance, ways to cultivate trust through consistency, and strategies to make security pertinent to the priorities of others.

Unlike other technical security texts that fixate on tools and frameworks, this book concentrates on the human factors that ultimately determine the effective use of those tools. It isn't about making readers feel smarter; it is about empowering them to become more influential. The stories selected were not intended to dazzle, but to educate, showcasing how real security professionals navigate the intricate dynamics of organizations to effect lasting change. Some narratives highlight brilliant technical minds who struggle with influence due to their inability to simplify their knowledge. Others feature less technically adept individuals who triumph through empathy, communication, and relationship cultivation.

The book's approach mirrors the enduring principles of Dale Carnegie, grounded in stories that illustrate behavioral change rather than mere knowledge accumulation. The aim is not to produce security experts who merely know more, but security influencers who achieve more. Each principle will build upon the last, fostering a journey from basic communication to strategic leadership. By the time you reach the final chapter, you will not only have a toolkit of techniques but also a transformed mindset regarding security's function and your potential impact.

* * *

I want readers to understand exactly what tools they will gain from each chapter.

Chapter 2: Speak Their Language, Not Your Expertise explores how technical language creates barriers instead of bridges. You'll learn practical translation techniques that transform security concepts into terms others can understand and act upon. This isn't about dumbing down, it's about making complex ideas accessible to drive action.

Chapter 3: Lead with Empathy, Not Alerts shows why understanding others' perspectives is your greatest security advantage. You'll see how security professionals transform resistance into partnership by starting with curiosity instead of controls. The chapter provides frameworks for practicing empathetic listening and framing security in terms of what matters to your stakeholders.

Chapter 4: Frame Security in Terms of Business Outcomes teaches you to speak the language of the boardroom. You'll discover how to translate technical metrics into business impact, quantify risk in financial terms, and align security initiatives with strategic priorities. The examples demonstrate how security professionals secure executive support by linking their work to revenue, cost, and competitive advantage.

Chapter 5: Build Trust Through Consistency, Not Control reveals why trust is your most valuable currency. You'll learn how security teams transform from enforcers to advisors through transparent communication and reliable follow-through. The chapter provides specific practices for building credibility in everyday interactions and during critical incidents.

Chapter 6: Make Security Their Idea, Not Your Mandate demonstrates the power of psychological ownership. You'll see how security professionals create enthusiastic advocates by involving others in solution development rather than imposing requirements. The techniques show you how to plant seeds that others will nurture and defend.

Chapter 7: Collaborate on Solutions, Don't Dictate Requirements builds on ownership by showing how co-creation leads to better security outcomes. You'll learn structured approaches for turning security reviews into design partnerships and how to facilitate productive collaboration across technical boundaries.

Chapter 8: Build Coalitions Before You Need Them reveals why your network is your net worth in security influence. You'll discover strategic approaches to relationship building that create informal channels of support and intelligence. The chapter shows how to map stakeholders and cultivate partnerships that transcend organizational silos.

Chapter 9: Navigate Politics with Awareness, Not Avoidance tackles the reality of organizational dynamics. You'll learn to map decision-making processes, understand competing priorities, and time your initiatives for maximum impact. The examples demonstrate how political intelligence improves effectiveness without compromising integrity.

Chapters 10 through 12 focus on operational excellence, managing workflow rather than just volume, designing security to be the path of least resistance, and building culture beyond mere awareness. These chapters provide frameworks for creating sustainable security practices that don't depend on constant enforcement.

The final chapters explore security leadership through clarity rather than authority, building organizational capability instead of dependency, and charting your path forward as a security influencer. These chapters complete your transformation from technical expert to trusted advisor and strategic partner.

Each chapter builds on the previous one, creating a progression from basic communication skills to strategic leadership. By the end, you'll have practical techniques for every situation where security requires influence, which is to say, every situation in security.

Before we move on, I want you to consider three questions.

First, when was the last time you felt frustrated that someone didn't understand or act on your security advice?

Second, what language were you speaking, your technical dialect or theirs?

And finally, what might change if you approached that conversation with translation rather than transmission in mind?"

Effective security isn't about being the smartest person in the room; it's about being the most understood. Your expertise becomes influential only when others can grasp and apply it. In the next chapter, we'll explore how to speak their language instead of expecting them to learn yours. Because when security professionals stop transmitting and start translating, we don't just change conversations, we change outcomes.

Chapter 2:
Speak Their Language,
Not Your Expertise

Maya gathered her team in the glass-walled conference room they'd nicknamed "The Fishbowl." The morning after the incident, everyone looked like they'd aged a year overnight. Priya rubbed her eyes behind thick-framed glasses. Aaron slouched in his chair, his usual energy depleted. Tina tapped furiously at her laptop, likely documenting the last of the incident details.

"Before we do the formal postmortem," Maya said, settling into a chair, "I want to talk about what really happened yesterday. Not the technical breakdown, we'll cover that later, but the communication breakdown."

The team exchanged glances. Maya noticed their confusion.

"Let me explain," she continued. "We had all the right technical responses. But somewhere between identifying the problem and getting others to act on it, we lost something crucial."

Priya straightened up. "You mean my presentation to the product team."

Maya nodded. "Walk us through what happened."

Priya winced. "I spent three days building that deck. Sixty-four slides of technical evidence showing exactly how the API vulnerability could be exploited. I included every CVSS score, attack vector analysis, and remediation option." She sighed. "And they just... stared at me. Then asked if we could 'circle back next sprint.'"

"The most technically comprehensive security presentation I've ever seen," Maya acknowledged. "And it went nowhere. Why?"

"Because they didn't understand a word of it," Aaron offered.

"It's more than that," Maya said. "They didn't see how it connected to what they care about. Priya, you spoke your language, not theirs."

Tina looked up from her laptop. "I've been there. Last month, I told Engineering their authentication system needed fixing. They nodded, said 'interesting,' and did nothing. Yesterday, I told them the same system was causing three-second load delays for users. They fixed it by the end of the day."

Maya smiled. "Exactly. You translated the security problem into performance impact, something they value and understand."

"But shouldn't they care about security for security's sake?" Priya asked, frustration evident.

"In an ideal world, maybe. But we don't secure systems in an ideal world, we secure them in this one," Maya replied. "Remember what happened with the SOC 2 compliance report last quarter?"

Aaron groaned. "God, yes. I sent that detailed matrix of controls to the CFO. Twenty pages of technical specifications. She called me an hour later, asking what it meant for the Acme contract."

"And once you told her it could delay closing their biggest deal..."

"She approved the security budget increase that afternoon," Aaron finished.

Maya stood and walked to the whiteboard. She wrote: TRANSLATE, DON'T TRANSMIT.

"This is the difference between being technically right and being influential. We're not dumbing down security, we're making it accessible. We're building bridges, not walls."

Priya looked thoughtful. "So for the product team, instead of vulnerability details..."

"Talk about how it affects release timelines," Tina suggested.

"Or customer trust metrics," Aaron added.

"Or competitive advantage," Maya said. "The security information doesn't change, but how we package it does. When we translate our expertise into their priorities, we don't just get heard, we get action."

The team nodded, energy returning to the room.

"Before our next meeting," Maya said, "I want each of you to reframe one security issue you're working on. Not in our language, but in the language of whoever needs to act on it. Remember: being the smartest person in the room doesn't matter if no one understands why they should listen."

* * *

Maya capped the dry-erase marker and studied her team's faces. The words "TRANSLATE, DON'T TRANSMIT" stood bold against the whiteboard, but she could see the concept hadn't fully landed yet.

TRANSLATE, DON'T TRANSMIT

"Let me ask you something," she said, leaning against the table. "How many years of specialized knowledge do each of you have?"

Aaron tilted his head. "Eight years in threat intelligence."

"Six in incident response," Tina offered.

Priya crossed her arms. "Twelve in SOC operations."

"That's twenty-six years of specialized security expertise in this room alone," Maya said. "And with that expertise comes a language, a dialect, that's second nature to us. We forget that others don't speak it."

She picked up her coffee mug, the one with the faded DEF CON logo. "When I first started as a systems architect, I thought the most technical person always won the argument. I'd overwhelm people with jargon until they gave in."

"That usually works," Priya muttered.

"It gets compliance, not commitment," Maya countered. "There's a difference. Compliance is 'fine, whatever you say.' Commitment is 'I understand why this matters.'"

She walked to the window overlooking the downtown skyline. Morning light caught the glass facades of neighboring buildings.

"Think about doctors," she continued. "The best ones don't tell patients about 'myocardial infarctions with ST elevation', they say 'your heart isn't getting enough oxygen.' Same information, different packaging."

Aaron nodded slowly. "I get that. But sometimes I feel like I'm... I don't know, betraying the technical truth when I simplify."

"It's not simplifying, it's translating," Maya said. "The rigor remains. We're just making it accessible."

Tina closed her laptop. "I've noticed something. When I use too much security jargon, people's eyes glaze over. It's like I've given them permission to tune out. Like I'm saying, 'This is too complex for you.'"

"Exactly," Maya said. "Jargon creates distance. And distance creates disengagement."

Priya shifted in her seat, her skepticism still evident. "But when I tried to explain things simply to the product team last month, they thought the issue wasn't serious."

"That's the challenge," Maya acknowledged. "We confuse precision with persuasion. You can be precisely right and completely ineffective."

She returned to the whiteboard and drew three columns: "Technical Truth," "Translation," and "Impact."

"Let's practice with Priya's presentation. What was the core technical issue?"

Priya straightened. "The API had no rate limiting, making it vulnerable to enumeration attacks."

Maya wrote this in the first column. "Now, translate that for a product manager."

The room fell silent. Finally, Aaron spoke up. "The login system lets attackers make unlimited guesses, which could lock out real users and expose their accounts."

Maya nodded, writing it down. "And the impact?"

"Customer complaints, support tickets, potential data breach headlines," Tina offered.

"Competitive disadvantage, our rivals all have this protection," Priya added, warming to the exercise.

As Maya filled in the columns, the energy in the room shifted. The team leaned forward, engaged.

"This is what translation looks like," she said. "We're not abandoning technical accuracy, we're wrapping it in relevance."

She set down the marker and faced her team. "Our security expertise is valuable, but it's trapped in our heads until we translate it. The most sophisticated detection means nothing if no one acts on it."

Priya studied the board, then looked at Maya with newfound respect. "So we're not dumbing down security. We're making it... accessible."

"And actionable," Maya added. "Because security that isn't understood isn't implemented."

She glanced at her watch. "We have the executive briefing in an hour. Let's practice translating our incident response. Not what we did, but why it matters to them."

For the first time that morning, Priya smiled. "I think I'm starting to speak their language."

TECHNICAL TRUTH	TRANSLATION	IMPACT
API HAD NO RATE LIMITING	LOGIN SYSTEM LETS ATTACKERS MAKE UNLIMITED GUESSES	• CUSTOMER COMPLAINTS, SUPPORT TICKETS • POTENTIAL DATA BREACH HEADLINES

* * *

Priya leaned forward, arms crossed on the table. "You want a translation failure? I've got one that still keeps me up at night."

Maya recognized the shadow that crossed Priya's face, a look she'd seen on countless security professionals who'd learned the hard way that being right wasn't enough.

"This was before we worked together," Priya said. "Last company, about three years ago. We detected a sophisticated campaign targeting our customer database. Not just random scanning, focused, persistent attempts."

"APT (Advanced Persistent Threat; large criminal network or state actor)?" Maya asked.

"Textbook case. I documented everything, the initial compromise vector, the lateral movement patterns, the data staging." Priya's fingers drummed against her forearm. "Put together what I thought was an airtight presentation. Forty-three slides of pure forensic gold."

Maya winced internally. She could already see where this was heading.

"I requested an emergency meeting with the leadership team. Got fifteen minutes at the end of their weekly sync." Priya shook her head. "I launched into the technical evidence, showed them packet captures, command and control traffic, data exfiltration attempts."

"How'd they respond?" Tina asked.

"The CEO interrupted me eight minutes in. Asked what I wanted them to do about it." Priya's voice tightened. "I told him we needed to take three critical systems offline for remediation, overhaul our network segmentation, and potentially notify customers."

The room fell quiet. Everyone knew what business leaders heard when security teams requested downtime, lost revenue, missed deadlines, and angry customers.

"He asked about the impact on operations," Priya continued. "I doubled down on the technical evidence, showed him more IOCs, more artifacts. Tried to explain the severity using the MITRE ATT&CK framework."

Maya nodded. "But that wasn't his currency."

"Not even close." Priya sighed. "Meeting ended with them asking me to 'monitor the situation' and 'come back when we had more certainty.'"

"What happened?" Aaron asked.

"Three weeks later, our customer data showed up on a dark web marketplace. Over two million records." Priya's eyes hardened. "The breach response cost eight figures. The CEO was out within six months."

Maya let the weight of the story settle. "And if you could go back to that meeting..."

"I'd skip the packet captures and IOCs entirely." Priya straightened. "I'd say: 'We have an active intruder who's stealing customer data that could cost us millions in remediation and lost business. Every day we wait increases that cost by approximately X dollars and Y percent customer churn.'"

"Their currency," Maya said quietly.

"Exactly." Priya nodded. "I was speaking security. They needed to hear risk and revenue."

* * *

"That's exactly the pattern," Maya said, leaning back in her chair. "We present evidence when we need to present outcomes."

Aaron cleared his throat. He'd been quiet through most of the discussion, his usual confidence seemingly dimmed. "I had my own translation failure last quarter with Marc."

Maya turned toward him, curious. Aaron rarely admitted to communication missteps; he took pride in being the team's bridge to other departments.

"The endpoint protection rollout?" Maya asked gently.

Aaron nodded, running a hand through his close-cropped hair. "I went in with this beautiful deck. Twenty slides breaking down EDR architecture, detection capabilities, and behavioral analysis algorithms. Even had this cool flowchart showing how the solution would integrate with our existing SIEM."

"Sounds comprehensive," Tina offered.

"It was technically flawless," Aaron said with a self-deprecating smile. "And a complete disaster. I lost Marc in the first three minutes."

Maya remembered that meeting. Marc Lindstrom, their CFO, had sat stone-faced through Aaron's presentation, his eyes occasionally flicking to his phone.

"He kept asking about licensing models and deployment timelines," Aaron continued. "I thought he was missing the point, so I doubled down on the technical superiority of the solution. Explained how the machine learning models worked and how the false positive rates compared to competitors."

"Let me guess," Priya interjected. "He wasn't impressed by your neural networks."

"Not even slightly." Aaron laughed. "He cut me off and said, and I'll never forget this, 'What's the dollar value of not doing this?'"

Maya nodded. That was pure Marc, always translating security requests into financial equations.

"I was completely thrown," Aaron admitted. "I had all these technical answers but no financial ones. The meeting ended with him asking me to 'rethink the business case' and come back when I could 'speak English, not security.'"

"So what changed?" Maya asked, though she already knew the answer. The endpoint protection project had eventually been approved with full funding.

"Pure luck," Aaron said. "I overheard Marc talking about the Westfield contract, that big healthcare deal we were finalizing. They were asking for security attestations, including endpoint protection specifics."

Maya watched understanding dawn on the faces around the table.

"So I went back to Marc with one slide," Aaron continued. "No technical specs, no architecture diagrams. Just three points: First, the Westfield deal required modern endpoint protection. Second, our competitors all had it. Third, implementing it would cost less than five percent of the deal's first-year value."

"And?" Tina prompted.

"Approved on the spot." Aaron shook his head in disbelief. "He even asked why we hadn't done it sooner."

Maya smiled. "Because you finally spoke his language. You gave him information he could understand and make a decision on"

"Exactly. I'd been selling security. He needed to hear revenue protection." Aaron's expression was thoughtful. "The weird part is, I didn't change the solution, just how I framed it. Same technology, same cost, same implementation plan."

"But completely different outcome," Maya noted. "That's the power of translation. It's not about dumbing down the technical reality, it's about elevating its relevance."

"The hardest part," Aaron added, "was realizing that my beautiful technical deck wasn't actually helping my case. I thought more detail meant more convincing."

"When actually..." Maya prompted.

Aaron nodded, the lesson clearly internalized. "When, actually, relevance beats detail every time. Marc didn't need to understand how the technology worked; he needed to understand why it mattered to his goals."

"And that," Maya said, "is the difference between speaking expertise and speaking influence."

* * *

"The translation challenge goes both ways," Maya said, turning her coffee mug slowly between her palms. "Sometimes the problem isn't over-explaining technical details. Sometimes it's making abstract risks feel concrete."

The team nodded, but Maya could see the question in their eyes. They wanted examples, not principles.

"Let me tell you about Jamie Chen." Maya smiled at the memory. "Best security architect I ever worked with, though she'd never call herself that."

Maya remembered Jamie's first week at FinSecure, back when Maya was still building her own reputation. The executive team had shot down three consecutive security proposals that quarter, each time citing "business priorities" as the reason.

"Jamie joined right after we'd been denied budget for API security scanning. The leadership team couldn't connect the dots between these invisible interfaces and actual business risk." Maya set her mug down. "Most architects would have come back with more technical evidence, penetration testing results, vulnerability counts, compliance requirements."

"That's what I would have done," Priya admitted.

"Jamie did something different. In her first executive briefing, she brought a set of house keys."

Maya could still picture Jamie standing before the executive team, dangling those keys. The CEO's confused expression. The COO's impatient glance at his watch.

She said, "Your APIs are like the keys to your house. You've built a beautiful home with expensive locks on the front door, but you're handing copies of your keys to every delivery person, landscaper, and visiting relative."

Maya paused, remembering how the room had shifted. How the executives had leaned forward almost in unison.

"Some of those keys open every door in the house. Some only open the garage. However, you don't have a record of which keys you've given out, who currently has them, or what they open. And you don't have a way to change the locks if someone makes a copy they shouldn't have."

Aaron whistled. "That's good."

"It was brilliant," Maya agreed. "In thirty seconds, she translated an abstract technical concept into something visceral and personal. Every executive in that room owned a home. Every one of them understood the risk of lost keys."

Maya remembered watching Jamie work the room, building on her metaphor with simple questions: Would you give your house key to someone without recording who has it? Would you use the same key for your front door and your safe? Would you notice if someone made an unauthorized copy?

"By the end of her fifteen-minute presentation, the CEO was asking why we hadn't implemented API security monitoring already. The same CEO who had rejected the proposal twice before."

"All because of a house key," Tina said.

"All because Jamie understood that technical truth isn't enough. You need emotional truth, too." Maya tapped the table for emphasis. "She didn't simplify the technical reality; she translated it into a language that triggered the right emotional response."

The team was quiet, absorbing the lesson.

"The most powerful part," Maya continued, "was that Jamie never positioned herself as the expert dispensing wisdom from on high. She was just helping them see what they already knew to be true. The risk wasn't theoretical anymore, it was as real as the keys in their pockets."

Maya thought about how she'd adapted this approach in her own career, finding metaphors that bridged the gap between security concepts and human experience.

"When we translate well, we're not just making ourselves understood. We're making our audience feel understood." Maya smiled at her team. "Jamie taught me that the best security communication doesn't showcase our expertise, it activates theirs."

* * *

Maya rose from her chair and walked to the whiteboard. She uncapped a marker and drew three simple columns.

"Let me give you some practical techniques for translation," she said, writing at the top of each column: "Storytelling," "Impact Mapping," and "Business-Aligned Metaphors."

Xander crossed his arms. "So we're just dumbing everything down now? Watering down the technical details until they're meaningless?"

Maya met his gaze. "Not at all. Think of it like code optimization. We're not removing functionality, we're making it more efficient for the target environment."

She tapped the first column. "Storytelling means framing technical concepts as narratives with characters, conflict, and resolution. Remember the breach at MediCore last year? Instead of saying 'insufficient access controls led to data exfiltration,' tell the story: 'An attacker found an unlocked door, spent three months exploring the building, and walked out with the crown jewels while everyone was watching the front entrance.'"

Several team members nodded, but Priya looked unconvinced.

Maya moved to the second column. "Impact mapping means connecting technical risks directly to business outcomes. Don't just say 'we need better API security.' Say 'our customer data pipeline has three unmonitored access points that could disrupt our revenue stream if compromised.'"

She wrote examples under each heading, watching as understanding began to dawn on their faces.

"The third technique is business-aligned metaphors. Find parallels to concepts the audience already understands. Network segmentation becomes neighborhood planning. Encryption becomes a secure courier service. Authentication becomes the VIP list at an exclusive club."

Tiffany raised her hand. "But what if they misunderstand the technical details because of the metaphor?"

"That's the breakthrough moment," Maya said. "You're not trying to make them security experts. You're trying to make them good decision-makers about security. Perfect technical understanding isn't the goal; appropriate action is."

Maya capped her marker. "This isn't about simplification, it's about amplification. You're not reducing the signal; you're cutting through the noise. When Jamie used those house keys, she didn't make the API risk less important; she made it more visible."

The room fell quiet as the team processed this shift in perspective.

"We've been thinking our expertise is what matters," Aaron said slowly. "But it's our ability to translate that expertise that actually creates change."

Maya smiled. "Exactly. Your technical knowledge isn't diminished by translation; it's magnified. Because knowledge that can't be acted upon might as well not exist."

Priya, who had been silent, finally spoke. "So we're not dumbing it down. We're lighting it up."

"Perfectly said," Maya replied. "Now let's practice with some real examples from our current projects."

PRACTICAL TECHNIQUES

STORYTELLING	IMPACT MAPPING	BUSINESS-ALIGNED METAPHORS
• An attacker found an unlocked door...	• Our customer data pipeline has three unmonitored access points...	Network segmenntation "Neighborhood planning" Encryption "A secure courier service"

* * *

Maya divided the team into pairs and observed them as they practiced translating complex security concepts. Their initial awkwardness gradually gave way to creative solutions and even laughter as metaphors took shape. She noticed how their body language had changed, becoming more open and animated.

After twenty minutes, she brought the group back together.

"Good work, everyone. But I want to emphasize something critical." Maya leaned against the whiteboard. "Being understood is just the foundation. It's necessary but not sufficient."

She drew a simple bridge on the board, connecting two points.

"Translation creates clarity, but connection creates action. When you speak their language, they hear you. But when you speak to what they care about, they follow you."

The marker squeaked as she added small figures on either side of the bridge.

"The next level is empathy, truly understanding the pressures, priorities, and perspectives of the person across from you." Maya's voice softened. "It's not just about making security understandable. It's about making it

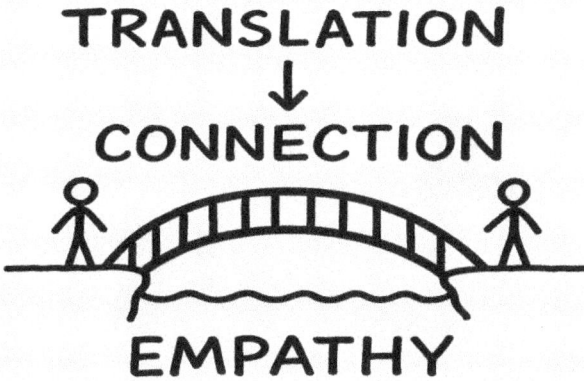

TRANSLATION
↓
CONNECTION

EMPATHY

matter in their world, not just ours."

She capped the marker and surveyed the room. "That's where we're heading next. Because when you combine clear translation with genuine empathy, you don't just inform decisions, you transform them."

Chapter 3:
Lead with Empathy, Not Alerts

Maya rolled her whiteboard marker between her fingers, considering her next words carefully. The training session had gone well, but theory only went so far. Her mind drifted to the Jenkins server incident from last month, a perfect case study in communication styles.

"Let me tell you about two incident reviews I've witnessed," she said. "Same type of security failure, completely different outcomes."

The room quieted. Even Priya, who had been checking her phone, looked up with interest.

"Three years ago at FinSecure, we had a major configuration error in our authentication system." Maya's voice took on a measured cadence as she recalled the scene. "Our CISO at the time, Jamie, ran the post-mortem like an interrogation. 'Who approved this change?' 'Why wasn't this documented?' 'How could you miss something so basic?'"

She drew a downward spiral on the whiteboard.

"By the end of that meeting, we had three things: a scapegoat, a new policy nobody would read, and a team that would never voluntarily report problems again." Maya paused, letting that sink in. "The next incident took twice as long to detect because nobody wanted to be the bearer of bad news."

Several team members exchanged knowing glances. They'd been there before.

"Last month, when our Jenkins server was compromised, Priya took a different approach." Maya nodded toward her SOC lead, who straightened slightly in her chair. "Instead of starting with 'who screwed up,' she asked: 'What pressures were you under when making these decisions? What information did you have, or not have? What would have helped?'"

Maya drew a bridge on the board, similar to her earlier diagram but with a different label: CURIOSITY.

"The team didn't just identify the technical fix; they uncovered the entire system that led to the vulnerability. The sprint deadline that rushed testing. The unclear documentation. The assumption that someone else was handling security reviews."

She capped her marker decisively.

"Fear-based security creates compliance without commitment. People follow the letter of the policy while looking for workarounds. But when you lead with empathy, with genuine curiosity about constraints and contexts, you get something more valuable: you get the truth."

Maya watched as understanding dawned across several faces. This wasn't just feel-good advice; this was operational strategy.

"Empathy isn't soft. It's pragmatic. It's how you get accurate information in high-stakes situations." She leaned forward slightly. "The most dangerous words in security aren't 'we've been hacked.' They're 'I was afraid to tell you.'"

Priya nodded almost imperceptibly, arms crossed but posture relaxed, a quiet acknowledgment.

"When people feel psychologically safe, they report problems earlier. They share near-misses. They ask questions instead of making assumptions." Maya walked toward the window, gathering her thoughts. "And those small moments of honesty are what prevent catastrophic failures."

She turned back to face the room.

"The technical skills in this room are exceptional. But they're worthless if people hide problems from us. Your ability to make others feel understood, not judged, is what determines whether you'll know about risks before or after they become incidents."

Maya let a moment of silence settle before concluding.

"So yes, translate your expertise clearly. However, remember that empathy isn't just about being nice. It's about being effective. It's how you build the trust that gives you access to the information you need most."

* * *

The training room emptied gradually, with nods of appreciation and murmured conversations trailing in Maya's wake. She gathered her notes, pleased with how the session had landed. The examples had resonated;

she could see it in their expressions, the subtle shift from polite attention to genuine engagement.

"That Jenkins example hit close to home."

Maya looked up to find Tina lingering by the door, laptop tucked under her arm. As the security architect for the payment processing team, Tina had a reputation for thoroughness that sometimes translated to rigidity.

"In a good way, I hope?" Maya asked.

"Yeah." Tina stepped back into the room, letting the door close. "Actually, I've been meaning to tell you about something that happened last month. Mind if I grab a coffee with you?"

Ten minutes later, they settled at a corner table in the building's café, away from the lunch rush crowd.

"Remember that API gateway project?" Tina stirred her latte absently. "The one where I kept getting pushback from the dev team?"

Maya nodded. The situation had been a classic standoff between security requirements and delivery timelines.

"I was ready to escalate. Had the email drafted and everything." Tina's laugh was self-deprecating. "Then I remembered what you said in that leadership workshop about asking questions instead of making statements."

"What happened?" Maya leaned forward slightly.

"I deleted the email. Went to their standup instead." Tina's eyes brightened with the memory. "Instead of saying 'Your authentication approach violates policy,' I asked what they were trying to accomplish with their design."

Maya smiled, recognizing the pivot.

"Turns out, they had legitimate concerns about latency that our standard approach would've made worse." Tina shook her head. "They weren't being difficult; they were solving a real problem. One I didn't even know existed."

"What did you do?"

"We whiteboarded for an hour. Found a solution that addressed both concerns." Tina's voice carried a note of wonder. "The lead developer actually thanked me afterward. Said it was the first time security felt like part of the team instead of the opposition."

Maya watched as understanding bloomed across Tina's face, the realization that empathy wasn't just interpersonal warmth, but a practical tool.

"The crazy part is what happened next," Tina continued. "Last week, they invited me to their design session for the new feature. Before I even asked. They wanted security input at the beginning."

"That's huge," Maya said quietly.

"It's like night and day. For years, I thought my job was to enforce standards." Tina's fingers traced patterns on the table. "Now I see that my actual leverage isn't in my authority, it's in my relationships."

Maya nodded. "When people feel understood, they stop hiding problems."

"Exactly. And they stop seeing security as the department of 'no.'" Tina's expression turned thoughtful. "It's funny, I always thought empathy was this soft skill that might make people like me more. I never saw it as something that would make me better at my actual job."

"That's the secret," Maya said. "Empathy isn't just about being nice. It's about understanding what matters to others, which gives you the influence to actually protect them effectively."

Tina gathered her things as they finished their coffees. "Thanks for creating that space today. I think a lot of us needed to hear it's okay to approach security differently."

Maya watched her go, noting the lighter step, the straightened shoulders. This was the transformation she valued most, not just changing practices, but changing perspectives as well. One conversation at a time, they were rebuilding what security meant to the organization.

Not a barrier, but a bridge.

* * *

Maya's phone buzzed as she walked back from the café. A calendar alert: the go-to-market strategy meeting for the new client portal was starting in five minutes. She quickened her pace, mentally shifting gears from her conversation with Tina.

The conference room hummed with pre-meeting tension when she arrived. Rina Patel stood at the whiteboard, marker in hand, sketching out what looked like a launch timeline. Luis Calderon sat nearby, scrolling through his phone with the intense focus of someone checking last-minute numbers.

"Maya! Perfect timing." Rina's greeting carried the clipped efficiency of someone with too many priorities. "We were just mapping the rollout for Apex."

Maya slid into an empty chair. The Apex client portal represented their biggest product launch of the quarter, and the most rushed. Three other team members were dialed in virtually, their faces arranged in squares on the wall screen.

"Where are we with the single sign-on integration?" Rina asked, adding another milestone to her timeline. "We need to lock this for the demo next week."

"That's actually why I wanted to join today," Maya said carefully. She'd reviewed the technical specs yesterday and spotted a concerning shortcut in the authentication flow. The kind that could lead to a credential compromise.

Luis looked up from his phone. "Apex is getting antsy. They've got three other vendors pitching next month, and their CIO specifically asked about the portal during our last call."

Maya felt the familiar pressure building in the room, the implicit message that security concerns were obstacles to overcome, not valid protections. The old Maya might have launched into an explanation of the authentication vulnerabilities, citing standards and best practices.

Instead, she asked, "What's driving the timeline on their end?"

Rina paused, marker hovering over the board. "Their fiscal year closes in six weeks. If they can't show progress on this initiative, they lose the budget allocation."

"And if we miss this window," Luis added, "they'll go with Meridian's solution. Which, between us, is garbage, but they're promising a thirty-day implementation."

Maya nodded, taking in their constraints. "That's a tough position. You've got sales pressure, they've got budget pressure, and everyone's feeling the clock."

Something in the room shifted slightly. Rina's shoulders relaxed a fraction.

"The SSO integration has some gaps," Maya continued. "But I think there's a way to address them without pushing the timeline."

Rather than listing the problems, she moved to the whiteboard. "What if we implement a phased approach? We could deploy the core functionality with added monitoring for the demo, then strengthen the authentication layer before full rollout."

Rina tilted her head, considering. "Would that satisfy the security requirements?"

"With the right guardrails, yes." Maya sketched a revised flow. "We'd need to limit initial access to test accounts and implement additional logging, but it keeps your demo on track while giving us time to properly secure the production environment."

Luis leaned forward. "So we're not saying no to the client?"

"We're saying yes, safely." Maya met his gaze. "I want this launch to succeed as much as you do. My job isn't to block progress, it's to make sure we don't compromise trust along the way."

Rina studied the revised plan, then nodded slowly. "This actually gives us a better story for the client. We can position the phased approach as extra diligence on their behalf."

"Exactly." Maya smiled. "And when their security team inevitably sends over their questionnaire, "

"We'll have solid answers instead of exceptions." Luis finished her thought, returning her smile. "Which means no ghosting after the security review."

As they refined the details, Maya felt the collaborative energy that emerged when security became a partner rather than a gatekeeper. By acknowledging their pressures instead of just asserting her own, she'd opened the door to a solution that protected everyone's interests.

The meeting concluded with a unified plan and genuine appreciation, rather than grudging compliance. As they filed out, Rina touched Maya's arm.

"Thanks for finding a path forward. Most security people would have just thrown up roadblocks."

"That's because they lead with alerts," Maya replied, "not empathy."

* * *

Maya gathered her tablet and notebook as the room emptied. The meeting's success still hummed in the air, that rare energy when technical needs and business priorities aligned rather than collided.

"How did you do that?"

Maya turned to find Jessica Huang hovering in the doorway, eyes wide with something between confusion and admiration. The security intern had been shadowing meetings all week.

"Do what exactly?" Maya asked, though she had a good idea what Jessica meant.

"That whole..." Jessica gestured vaguely at the whiteboard where the revised implementation plan remained. "You walked in, they were clearly going to bulldoze right over security concerns, and somehow you left with them thanking you for your input. I've been watching security-dev interactions for weeks now, and they usually end with someone storming out or passive-aggressive emails."

Maya smiled. "I asked what mattered to them before telling them what mattered to me."

"But, " Jessica's brow furrowed. "The authentication flow is still problematic."

"It is. And now we have a path to fix it that everyone's invested in." Maya nodded toward the hallway. "Walk with me? I'm meeting Tina for coffee."

They found Tina waiting in the small café area, already nursing a steaming mug. Her eyes brightened when she spotted them.

"Brought company?" Tina asked, pulling out a chair.

"Jessica's trying to figure out how security people can stop being the department of 'no' without compromising on actual security," Maya explained, setting down her things.

Tina laughed. "Oh, I remember those days. My first year in AppSec, the dev teams used to literally hide when they saw me coming."

Jessica slid into a seat. "What changed?"

"I stopped leading with mandates and started asking questions." Tina wrapped her hands around her mug. "There was this frontend team working on a customer dashboard. They kept implementing features without proper input validation, a classic injection vulnerability waiting to happen."

Maya nodded, having heard pieces of this story before.

"I'd been sending them increasingly annoyed tickets, citing OWASP guidelines, escalating to their manager." Tina shook her head at the memory. "Nothing worked. So finally, I just went over and asked them: 'What's making it hard to implement the validation controls?'"

"What did they say?" Jessica leaned forward.

"Turns out they had a legacy framework that made proper validation a nightmare. They weren't ignoring security, they were drowning in technical debt with impossible deadlines." Tina's expression softened. "Once I understood that, we worked together on a validation library that actually fit their constraints. Took two weeks instead of fighting for six months."

Maya smiled. "Curiosity before control."

"Exactly. After that, I began every security conversation with questions rather than requirements. 'What are you trying to accomplish?' 'What's your biggest challenge right now?' 'How might security support your goals?'" Tina took a sip of her coffee. "My relationships completely transformed. Teams started inviting me to planning sessions instead of dreading my reviews."

Jessica looked thoughtful. "But don't you sometimes need to just say no? Some risks are too big."

"Absolutely," Maya interjected. "But 'no' lands differently when it comes after understanding. It becomes 'I see what you're trying to do, and here's why this approach creates risk we can't accept, but let's find another way to meet your need.'"

Tina nodded. "The magic happens when they realize you're genuinely trying to help them succeed, not just enforce rules. Security becomes a collaborative challenge, not an opposing force."

"That's the difference between compliance and commitment," Maya added. "You can force compliance through authority, but you earn commitment through empathy."

Jessica's expression shifted from skepticism to consideration. "So it's not about softening the security requirements."

"Never," Tina said firmly. "It's about hardening the relationships so the requirements can actually take root."

* * *

"Let's head over to the SOC," Maya suggested, finishing her coffee. "I want you to see empathy in action during incident response. Priya runs a masterclass in it."

They walked across the building to the Security Operations Center, where analysts sat before glowing monitors displaying dashboards of alerts, network flows, and log data. Priya stood behind one of the analysts, reviewing something on their screen.

"Speak of the devil," Priya said, looking up. "I was just about to message you."

"Everything okay?" Maya asked.

"False positive. But a good teaching moment." Priya gestured them over. "Jessica, right? The intern?"

Jessica nodded, clearly awed by the SOC environment.

"We had an incident last month," Priya explained. "Potential data exfiltration from Finance. Everyone was pointing fingers, IT blamed the finance team for clicking something, and finance blamed IT for inadequate protection."

"What happened?" Jessica asked.

"That's what makes this story interesting," Maya said. "My predecessor would have launched straight into finding who to blame. Instead, Priya focused on understanding what happened."

Priya nodded. "I asked everyone to walk me through their normal workflow. It turns out that Finance was using an approved third-party tool that IT didn't recognize in the logs. The alerts were legitimate, but the activity wasn't malicious."

"The key was how Priya handled it," Maya added. "No accusations, just curiosity."

"After that incident, our reporting improved dramatically," Priya said. "People started coming to us earlier with concerns because they knew they wouldn't get blamed. They'd get help."

"Trust creates visibility," Maya summarized. "And visibility is our best defense."

An analyst waved to get Priya's attention about an emerging alert. As Priya excused herself, Maya suddenly felt a familiar pressure in her bladder.

"Excuse me a moment," Maya said, glancing at her empty coffee mug. "Too much caffeine. I need to handle my own incident response."

Jessica looked momentarily confused, then laughed as understanding dawned.

"Take your time," Tina said with a knowing smile. "We'll walk Jessica through some of the dashboards. They're a perfect example of how we've evolved from focusing on technical metrics to business impact."

Maya hurried down the hallway, reflecting on the irony. Even the most sophisticated security systems needed occasional human maintenance, a humbling reminder that beneath all the technical complexity, people remained at the center of security.

When Maya returned from the restroom, she found Jessica sitting beside Priya at the analyst station, watching intently as Priya walked her through something on the screen. The intern's face showed that mixture of concentration and awe that Maya recognized from her own early days in security.

"So you really don't get angry when people make mistakes?" Jessica was asking.

Priya looked up briefly as Maya approached, then turned back to Jessica. "Anger is just fear wearing a mask. When I first started in security, I was terrified of missing something critical, so I channeled that into being harsh with others."

"What changed?" Jessica leaned forward.

"Experience," Priya said, adjusting her blue-light glasses. "And a good mentor. I realized that fear closes communication channels, and in security, visibility is everything." She gestured toward the monitors. "These tools only show us what we know to look for. The human network tells us what we don't know yet."

Maya hung back, letting the conversation flow. This was exactly the kind of mentoring moment security needed more of.

"But how do you actually practice empathy?" Jessica pressed. "It sounds great in theory, but when I'm dealing with a developer who's ignoring security requirements..."

"Start with questions, not statements," Priya said, turning her chair to face Jessica fully. "When someone's resisting security measures, I begin with: 'What are you trying to accomplish?' Not 'Why aren't you following protocol?'"

Jessica nodded slowly. "So you're focusing on their goals first."

"Exactly. Most people aren't actively trying to create risk. They're trying to solve a problem, and security feels like it's in the way." Priya pulled out her notebook. "Let me show you my cheat sheet for empathetic security conversations."

She sketched a quick framework on a blank page:

"The key," Priya continued, "is that you're not pretending to care about their problems, you genuinely need to care. Empathy isn't a technique; it's a mindset."

"But doesn't that make you a pushover?" Jessica asked.

Priya laughed. "The opposite. When people know I understand their challenges, they're more willing to hear my concerns. Empathy gives me more influence, not less."

"It's like a Trojan horse," Maya added, finally joining the conversation. "But instead of sneaking in soldiers, you're sneaking in understanding."

"I prefer to think of it as building a bridge," Priya countered with a slight smile. "Soldiers suggest combat. Security isn't about winning battles, it's about reducing friction."

An alert pinged on Priya's screen, and she glanced at it briefly before continuing.

"The most powerful question in my arsenal is simple: 'What would make this easier for you?' When I ask that, I'm not compromising security. I'm finding a path that works for both of us."

Jessica looked thoughtful. "At school, they taught us all about controls and frameworks, but nothing about this."

"That's because technical skills get you hired," Priya said, "but people skills get you heard. Start practicing now. Next time you're in a security discussion, count to five before speaking, just to make sure you've fully heard the other person."

Maya watched Jessica absorb this wisdom, remembering her own journey from technical expert to influencer. The hardest lesson wasn't learning the technical skills, it was learning when not to lead with them.

* * *

Maya watched as Jessica's brow furrowed slightly. The intern's expression was one she'd seen countless times before, skepticism masked as consideration.

"But does this actually work in the real world?" Jessica finally asked. "I mean, security is about hard facts and controls."

Priya exchanged a knowing glance with Maya before turning back to Jessica. "You know what's fascinating? These are the exact same principles behind effective social engineering."

Jessica's eyes widened. "Wait, what?"

"Think about it," Priya continued, leaning forward. "What makes a good social engineer successful? They don't lead with technical jargon or demands. They establish rapport, they listen, they find pain points, and they position themselves as helpers."

Maya nodded. "The best attackers understand human psychology better than they understand technology. They know empathy is a pathway to influence."

"This isn't some new-age concept," Priya added. "Dale Carnegie documented these principles almost a century ago. His research showed that understanding others' perspectives before sharing your own is fundamental to influence. It's the foundation of 'How to Win Friends and Influence People.'"

Jessica looked between them. "So we're using the attackers' playbook?"

"We're using human psychology," Maya clarified. "The difference is our intent. We're building trust to improve security, not exploit it."

Priya closed her notebook. "The research is clear: empathy makes you smarter, not softer. When you understand someone's actual concerns, not what you assume they are, you can address the real barriers."

"And people open up when they feel understood," Maya added. "They share the workarounds they've been using, the shortcuts they've discovered. That visibility is invaluable intelligence for security."

Jessica seemed to be processing this. "So empathy isn't just being nice."

"It's strategic," Maya confirmed. "It gives you information you wouldn't otherwise have access to. It helps you anticipate resistance before it happens."

"And most importantly," Priya said, checking her watch, "it transforms security from something people work around into something people work with."

Maya stood, signaling the conversation was wrapping up. "The key takeaway is simple: technical expertise opens the door, but empathy gets you a seat at the table. When people feel understood, they're ready to listen."

Jessica nodded slowly. "I think I get it. It's not about being soft, it's about being smart about how humans actually work."

"Exactly," Maya smiled. "Now, let's move on to something equally important: how to build allies across the organization. Because empathy is just the beginning."

* * *

Jessica's eyes narrowed, her skepticism returning. "There's more of this woo-woo stuff?"

41

Maya couldn't help but smile. She remembered having the same reaction early in her career, the instinctive resistance to anything that didn't involve code or controls. She leaned against the conference room table, crossing her arms casually.

"I had the same thought when I was starting out," Maya said. "I was convinced that technical excellence was the only currency that mattered. Then I hit a wall."

"What kind of wall?" Jessica asked, her curiosity clearly piqued despite her skepticism.

"I'd built this incredible security architecture for a financial services company. Perfect controls, defense in depth, amazing detection capabilities." Maya paused, remembering the frustration. "And then the CTO shelved the entire project."

"Why would they do that?" Jessica looked genuinely confused.

"Because I hadn't connected it to what they actually cared about." Maya moved back to her chair and sat down. "I built what I thought was important, not what served their business priorities."

Priya nodded knowingly. "Classic security mistake."

"Understanding people is the first step; understanding their business goals is the next," Maya continued. "Every company exists to do something specific, make money, serve customers, solve problems. Security only matters to them if it helps with those goals."

Jessica frowned. "But security is important regardless."

"To us, yes. But we're not the ones making budget decisions." Maya pulled out her notebook and sketched a quick diagram. "Look at it this way: when you're advocating for security, you're competing for limited resources against people who are promising revenue growth, customer satisfaction, or market expansion."

"So we lose," Jessica said flatly.

"Not if we frame security in terms of those same business objectives." Maya tapped her pen on the paper. "When I redid my pitch to that CTO, I didn't talk about threats or vulnerabilities. I talked about how my solution would accelerate their compliance certification, which would unlock a new market segment worth millions."

"And they approved it?"

"They increased the budget," Maya said with a small smile. "Because suddenly security wasn't competing with business objectives, it was enabling them."

Priya gathered her things. "That's why the next session will be critical. We'll show you how to map security initiatives to business priorities."

Jessica looked thoughtful. "So it's not just about speaking their language or understanding their feelings. It's about actually connecting what we do to what they need."

"Exactly," Maya nodded, pleased with Jessica's quick understanding. "Security for security's sake is a hard sell. Security that enables business outcomes gets funded."

"I think I get it now," Jessica said, her earlier skepticism fading. "This isn't woo-woo stuff at all. It's strategy."

"The most effective kind," Maya confirmed, standing up. "When you align with business goals, you're not just getting approval, you're building lasting partnerships across the organization."

As they prepared to leave, Maya felt a familiar sense of satisfaction. These conversations always reminded her of her own journey from technical specialist to strategic leader. The technical skills had opened doors, but it was understanding people and business that had ultimately made her effective.

"We'll pick this up tomorrow," Maya said, holding the door. "Get some rest. The next part is where things really get interesting."

Jessica nodded, a new determination in her eyes. "I'll be ready."

As they parted ways in the hallway, Maya made a mental note to share some specific examples tomorrow. The transition from empathy to business alignment was where many promising security professionals stumbled. But based on today's conversation, she had high hopes for Jessica.

Chapter 4:

Frame Security in Terms of Business Outcomes

Maya surveyed the executive boardroom as she set up her presentation. The quarterly security budget meeting always brought mixed emotions, opportunity, and anxiety tangled together like crossed wires. The sleek mahogany table reflected the overhead lights, making the room seem even more intimidating than it was.

Elena Park, the CEO, was already seated at the head of the table, reviewing something on her tablet with a furrowed brow. Marc Lindstrom, the CFO, was setting up his laptop, his expression carefully neutral. Tariq Bashir, the CTO, was engaged in quiet conversation with Rina Patel from Product. Ken Willis, the VP of IT, sat stiffly in his usual spot, his posture radiating territorial defensiveness.

Maya had brought Jessica along, partly for the experience, partly because Jessica's dashboard prototype was part of today's presentation. The intern looked both excited and terrified, clutching her notebook like a shield.

"Let's begin," Elena said, glancing at her watch. "Maya, you're requesting a fifteen percent budget increase for next quarter. That's ambitious in our current climate."

Maya nodded, clicking to her first slide. "I understand the timing is challenging. But I believe this investment is critical to our business objectives."

Ken Willis cleared his throat. "We've managed fine with current resources. I'm not seeing the justification for such a significant increase."

Maya recognized the familiar dance beginning. She'd seen it at FinSecure, at Meridian, and now here at TechForward. Security teams are talking about vulnerabilities while executives are thinking about valuations. Two entirely different languages, with the budget hanging in the balance.

"If I may," Maya said, skipping ahead several slides to one titled 'Business Impact.' "I'd like to frame this differently than we have in the past."

On the screen appeared not the usual vulnerability metrics or threat statistics, but a simple chart showing three business outcomes: Time-to-Market, Customer Trust Indicators, and Revenue Protection.

"Our security program isn't just about preventing bad things," Maya continued. "It's about enabling TechForward to move faster, build deeper customer trust, and protect our revenue streams."

Marc Lindstrom sat up straighter, his attention captured. "Go on."

"The Apex client portal represents our biggest product launch this quarter," Maya said, nodding toward Rina. "Our current security processes would add three weeks to the timeline. The tools and staffing I'm requesting would cut that to three days while maintaining our security standards."

Rina's eyebrows shot up. "Three days instead of three weeks? That would completely change our release cadence."

"Exactly," Maya said. "We're not asking for budget to block progress, we're asking for resources to accelerate it safely."

Luis Calderon, who had slipped in late, leaned forward. "What about the trust indicators? We've lost three enterprise deals this month because of security questionnaire responses."

"That's the second component," Maya replied, advancing to a slide showing competitive analysis. "Our competitors are using security as a differentiator. The dashboard Jessica has prototyped would give our sales team real-time access to compliance status and security metrics that matter to customers."

Jessica straightened in her seat as all eyes turned to her briefly.

"Rather than talking about CVEs or patch rates," Maya continued, "we're focusing on metrics that directly impact sales cycles and customer confidence."

Ken Willis scoffed. "This sounds like a lot of repackaging of basic security functions."

Tariq shot him a look. "No, Ken, this is different. Maya's talking about security as a business enabler, not just a cost center."

Marc was studying the financial projections. "These numbers suggest the investment would pay for itself within two quarters through accelerated sales cycles alone."

"That's correct," Maya confirmed. "When we frame security in terms of business outcomes rather than just technical vulnerabilities, the ROI becomes much clearer."

Elena had been quiet, observing the room dynamics. Now she spoke. "I appreciate this approach, Maya. It's the first time I've seen security presented as a growth strategy rather than just risk mitigation."

Maya felt a small victory. She'd learned this lesson the hard way at previous companies: talking about vulnerabilities got you polite nods, while talking about value got you a budget. Security teams often focused on what could go wrong, while executives focused on what could go right. The bridge between them wasn't technical; it was financial.

"There's one more component," Maya said, advancing to the final slide. "Revenue protection."

The room grew quieter as she outlined how the security investments would safeguard their existing revenue streams from disruption, regulatory penalties, and reputation damage.

"In summary," Maya concluded, "this isn't about buying tools to fix vulnerabilities. It's about investing in capabilities that will accelerate our time-to-market, strengthen our competitive position, and protect our revenue streams."

As the discussion continued, Maya caught Jessica watching her intently. The intern was witnessing firsthand what Maya had tried to explain yesterday, security translated into business language became not just tolerable, but valuable.

The meeting wouldn't result in everything Maya wanted; budget negotiations never did. But by framing security in terms of business outcomes rather than technical threats, she'd changed the conversation from "Why do we need this?" to "How quickly can we implement it?"

And that shift, Maya knew, was worth more than any single budget line item could ever be.

* * *

Maya slipped her tablet into her bag as the meeting concluded, pleased with the shift in energy she'd created. She gathered her notes while several executives lingered, continuing discussions about implementation timelines rather than questioning the necessity of the security program itself.

"That was..." Jessica struggled to find words as they stepped into the hallway. "I didn't know you could talk about security like that."

Maya smiled. "Like what?"

"Like a business person. Not a security person." Jessica's expression was a mixture of confusion and admiration. "In my courses, we only focused on the technical aspects, vulnerabilities, threats, and controls."

"Which are all important," Maya acknowledged, "but insufficient on their own."

Elena and Tariq caught up with them, Elena gesturing toward her office. "Maya, do you have a few minutes? I'd like to continue our discussion."

In Elena's corner office, with its view of the downtown skyline, Tariq closed the door behind them. "That was masterful," he said. "You completely reframed the conversation."

Elena nodded. "Where did you learn to speak MBA? Most security leaders I've worked with couldn't translate technical value to save their lives."

Maya leaned against the conference table. "Necessity. After my third budget request was denied at FinSecure, I realized I needed to speak the language of the people holding the purse strings."

"So you went back to school?" Jessica asked.

"Not exactly. I took some free online courses from Harvard Business School online. Watched countless YouTube videos on corporate finance and business strategy. Eventually convinced the company to send me to a business essentials program." Maya smiled. "I even joined a local Toastmasters group that happened to be full of MBAs. Best education I ever got."

Tariq laughed. "That explains a lot."

"What I learned," Maya continued, "is that businesses fundamentally care about five things: revenue growth, profit margins, customer retention, market share, and shareholder value. Everything else is just a means to those ends."

Jessica frowned. "But security doesn't directly increase any of those."

"That's where you're wrong," Maya said gently. "Security directly impacts all of them, just not always in the way we think."

Maya walked to the whiteboard and drew a simple diagram. "Take revenue growth. Security enables faster deployment of new products because we build safe pipelines rather than becoming bottlenecks. We protect existing revenue streams by preventing outages and breaches that would drive customers away."

"And profit margins," Elena added. "A breach costs exponentially more than prevention."

"Exactly," Maya nodded. "The average cost of a data breach is $4.45 million. That's straight off the bottom line. When I present security as margin protection rather than just risk reduction, CFOs suddenly get very interested."

Maya continued her diagram. "Customer retention is perhaps the most directly impacted. Trust is the foundation of customer relationships, and security is the foundation of trust. When we quantify the customer lifetime value and multiply it by improved retention rates through stronger security postures, the numbers become compelling."

Jessica was taking notes furiously. "This was never covered in my training."

"Because most security training focuses on the how, not the why," Tariq said.

"Market share is similar," Maya continued. "When TechForward can demonstrate better security than competitors, it becomes a differentiator. That's why I emphasized the dashboard for the sales team, it turns our security posture into a competitive advantage."

Elena studied the diagram. "And shareholder value?"

"That's the culmination of all the others," Maya explained. "When security prevents the stock drop that typically follows a breach, an average of 5% long-term, we're directly protecting market capitalization. When we enable faster, safer product launches, we're supporting growth narratives that drive valuations."

Jessica looked up from her notes. "So it's not just about preventing bad things."

"Never has been," Maya said. "Security's true value is in enabling good things to happen, safely and confidently. That's the language of business, and that's how we get budgets approved."

* * *

"But how do you actually come up with this stuff?" Jessica asked, her expression caught between admiration and bewilderment. "These metrics and financial impacts, they seem so... natural when you present them."

Maya smiled, thinking back to her early days at TechForward. "I cheated," she admitted.

Tariq raised an eyebrow. "Cheated?"

"I made friends with the money people." Maya leaned against the window, watching the afternoon light play across the skyline. "When I first got here, I noticed something interesting. The CFO, CRO, and CMO always had lunch together on Wednesdays. Sometimes the COO would join them."

"The revenue crew," Elena nodded. "Marc's inner circle."

"Exactly. They're essentially the company's engine room; they make the numbers work. I wanted to be in that conversation." Maya's voice softened with the memory. "So I started showing up at their table. Not every week, just occasionally. I'd ask questions about their challenges, what metrics they tracked, and how they measured success. Sometimes we even talked about our kids."

"That's... bold," Jessica said.

"It was terrifying," Maya laughed. "But I realized something important. Security was a black box to them, and their world was a black box to me. We were speaking completely different languages."

Maya walked back to the whiteboard. "The Gray Hat taught me this at my last company. He said, 'Maya, if you were going to Mexico, would you insist everyone there speak English, or would you learn some Spanish?'"

"The Gray Hat?" Jessica looked confused.

"A mentor. Enigmatic individual, former Red Teamer turned executive whisperer. He had this way of cutting through complexity with these perfect analogies." Maya smiled at the memory. "His point was simple: you speak Pashtu in Afghanistan, not Peru. You speak French in France, not Finland. Languages exist in specific contexts."

"And business metrics are the language of the executive suite," Tariq concluded.

"Precisely. The Gray Hat told me, 'Security professionals often act like tourists who are angry that locals don't understand them.'" Maya capped her marker. "So I started learning their language. I'd ask Marc about EBITDA and customer acquisition costs. I asked Luis about sales cycles and deal velocities. I learned what made their world turn."

"That's why your presentations feel different," Elena said. "You're not translating security into business terms, you're actually thinking in business terms."

"It took time," Maya admitted. "But eventually, I could walk into any meeting and frame security in the language of whoever was in the room. With Finance, I discuss ROI and risk-adjusted return. With Sales, I talk about competitive differentiation and deal acceleration. With Marketing, I talk brand protection and trust signaling."

Jessica was scribbling furiously again. "So for the dashboard transformation..."

"Exactly. Our current dashboards speak security language, vulnerabilities, patches, and compliance rates. But the executive team needs a dashboard that speaks their language, revenue protected, speed to market, and customer trust metrics." Maya's eyes lit up. "That's our next project. We're going to rebuild our entire measurement framework around business outcomes, not security activities."

"The Gray Hat would be proud," Tariq said.

Maya nodded, remembering her mentor's words: Don't fight for a seat. Earn one by making others feel seen. "He also taught me something else important, the reason to learn their language isn't just to get what you want. It's to truly understand their world. When you do that, you start to see how security can actually help them succeed, not just avoid failure."

Elena stood, signaling the meeting's end. "Well, I'm glad you learned to speak our language, Maya. It's made all the difference."

"The funny thing is," Maya said as they walked toward the door, "once you learn to speak their language, they become much more interested in learning yours."

* * *

Maya caught the subtle glance Elena gave toward her laptop, recognizing the CEO's carefully masked impatience. Years of reading executive body language had taught her when a meeting had reached its natural conclusion.

"Thank you for making time for us, Elena," Maya said, gathering her tablet. "I know your schedule is packed today. We'll get out of your hair so you can prep for the investor call."

Elena's shoulders relaxed slightly. "How did you know about the call?"

"The calendar tells stories if you know how to read it," Maya smiled. "Your afternoon blocks have that specific shade of 'don't interrupt me' blue."

They exchanged knowing looks as Maya ushered Jessica toward the door. Tariq had already slipped out, heading back to his desk.

As they walked down the hallway toward the security wing, Jessica hurried to keep pace with Maya's purposeful stride.

"That was amazing how you wrapped up without making it awkward," Jessica said. "But I'm still trying to understand the dashboard strategy. How do you actually connect security metrics to business outcomes?"

Maya slowed her pace. "Think of it as a translation matrix. On one axis, we have our security metrics, mean time to detect, vulnerability density, and security debt. On the other axis, we have business outcomes, revenue, customer acquisition, and market share."

She pulled out her phone and opened a simple spreadsheet. "See this? For each security metric, I've mapped the business impact. Take mean time to remediate critical vulnerabilities. In security-speak, that's about reducing exposure time. In business-speak, it's about reducing the window where a breach could disrupt operations and impact quarterly earnings."

Jessica studied the screen. "So you're essentially creating a Rosetta Stone between security and business."

"Exactly. And the key is to start with the business outcome, not the security metric. Ask yourself: What does the business care about right now? Is it launching a new product? Entering a new market? Reducing operational costs?"

They paused at the water cooler.

"Once you know that," Maya continued, filling a paper cup, "you can identify which security metrics directly support those goals. If they're focused on product launches, we highlight how our security review velocity impacts time-to-market. If they're worried about operational costs, we show how our automation reduces security-related delays."

Jessica nodded slowly. "So we're not just reporting numbers, we're telling a story about how security enables business success."

"Now you're getting it," Maya smiled. "Security isn't the end goal. It's the enabler of trust, and trust drives business value. That's the language that gets you not just a seat at the table, but a voice that people actually want to hear."

* * *

Maya and Jessica pushed through the double doors leading to the security wing, where the harsh fluorescent lighting stood in stark contrast to the soft recessed LEDs in the executive suites. They found the team already gathered in their modest conference room, affectionately dubbed "The Bunker" by Priya, for the weekly security architecture review.

Aaron, their newest security architect, was midway through a presentation as they slipped in. Maya noticed his slide, which showed a neatly organized risk assessment matrix with dollar figures prominently displayed next to each category.

"Perfect timing," Priya said, glancing up from her notes. "Aaron was just explaining how he convinced Product to drop that new analytics vendor they were pushing for."

Aaron, a former developer who'd transitioned to security six months ago, nodded. "It wasn't easy. Rina was pretty set on this vendor; they had all the machine learning capabilities Product wanted for the Apex client portal."

"But you managed to change her mind," Maya said, settling into a chair. "That's no small feat."

Aaron clicked to the next slide. "I did what you taught us, I spoke their language. Instead of just listing CVEs or talking about their poor authentication model, I quantified what a breach would actually cost us."

The slide showed a simple but powerful breakdown: revenue impact from service disruption, remediation costs, regulatory fines, and, most importantly, projected customer churn based on similar incidents in their industry.

"The key was showing them that a data leak through this vendor would cost us approximately 8% of our annual revenue, $4.2 million, plus erode the trust we've built with the finance clients we just signed."

Jessica leaned forward. "And they actually listened to that?"

"They did more than listen," Aaron said with a hint of pride. "Rina asked me to help evaluate alternative vendors that could meet their needs without the security gaps. We're partnering on the selection now."

Maya smiled. "That's exactly the approach we need. You didn't just say no, you showed them why it mattered in terms they care about, then offered to help find a path forward."

"It's like you keep telling us," Aaron said. "Security without business context is just noise. When I framed it as protecting revenue instead of blocking progress, suddenly I wasn't the bad guy anymore. I was the one helping them avoid a costly mistake."

Priya raised her coffee mug in a mock toast. "And that, Jessica, is how we're becoming business bilingual around here. We're not just security people anymore, we're business risk translators."

* * *

Jessica leaned forward, tucking a strand of hair behind her ear. "So, how exactly do you do that translation? I get the concept, but when I'm looking at a vulnerability report or threat assessment, I don't automatically see dollar signs."

Maya nodded, understanding the gap between concept and execution. She pulled a blank whiteboard closer. She has trained everyone to have whiteboards nearby at all times.

"Let me give you a crash course. Think of it as learning to speak a second language." She uncapped a marker. "Business leaders care about five main things: revenue, costs, productivity, competitive advantage, and reputation. Our job is to translate security concepts into one or more of these categories."

She wrote these five terms across the top of the board. "First, you need to understand the basic financial metrics that matter to executives."

Maya drew a simple chart below. "ROI, return on investment. This isn't just 'we need this security tool.' It's 'this $200,000 investment prevents an estimated $1.2 million in breach costs, giving us a 6x return.'"

"Next is TCO, total cost of ownership. Don't just calculate the purchase price of security solutions; also consider the total cost of ownership. Include implementation time, training, maintenance, and the operational overhead for other teams."

Jessica scribbled notes. "What about quantifying risks? That seems like the hardest part."

"Great question. Start with the Annual Loss Expectancy formula." Maya wrote on the board: "ALE = Single Loss Expectancy × Annual Rate of Occurrence."

"If a type of security incident typically costs $100,000 to remediate, and based on industry data, it happens to companies like ours about 0.3 times per year, the ALE is $30,000. This helps prioritize where to invest."

Priya jumped in. "Don't forget opportunity cost. When I present to Elena, I always calculate what the business can't do if security blocks them versus what they risk losing in a breach."

"Exactly," Maya agreed. "And for publicly traded companies, consider stock impact. The average company loses 5-7% of market value after a significant breach disclosure."

Aaron nodded. "That's what clinched it with Rina. When I showed her that similar breaches had caused competitors to lose customers to us, she immediately got it."

Maya drew a diagram showing concentric circles. "I use this model. Start with direct costs at the center: incident response, forensics, legal fees, and customer notification. Then add indirect costs, productivity loss, reputation damage, customer churn, and regulatory fines."

She turned to Jessica. "The key is connecting these numbers to the specific business context. Don't just say 'security matters.' Say 'this vulnerability in the Apex portal puts $3.2 million of annual recurring revenue at risk because it affects our highest-value financial clients.'"

"And when you're not sure about the exact numbers?" Jessica asked.

"Use ranges and comparables. Say 'Based on similar incidents in our industry, this type of breach typically costs between $800,000 and $1.2 million.' It's better to be approximately right than precisely wrong."

Maya capped her marker. "Remember, you're not just calculating numbers, you're telling a financial story about risk. The math matters, but so does the narrative about what these numbers mean to the business."

Jessica looked at her notes. "So instead of saying 'we need better authentication,' I should say 'implementing MFA would reduce account takeover risk by 80%, protecting $500,000 in annual revenue from our enterprise clients.'"

Maya smiled. "You're already getting it. When you speak their language, you're not just the security person anymore, you're a business partner helping protect what matters most. Just make sure to do your homework because they'll want receipts."

ALIGNING SECURITY WITH BUSINESS METRICS

REVENUE	COSTS	PRODUCTIVITY	COMPETITIVE ADVANTAGE

$$ROI \rightarrow \frac{investment}{benefit}$$

$$ALE$$
$$SLE \times ARO$$

RISK QUANTIFICATION

TCO
purchase
maintenance
operations

TCO
purchase
maintenance
operations

RISK
QUANTIFICATION

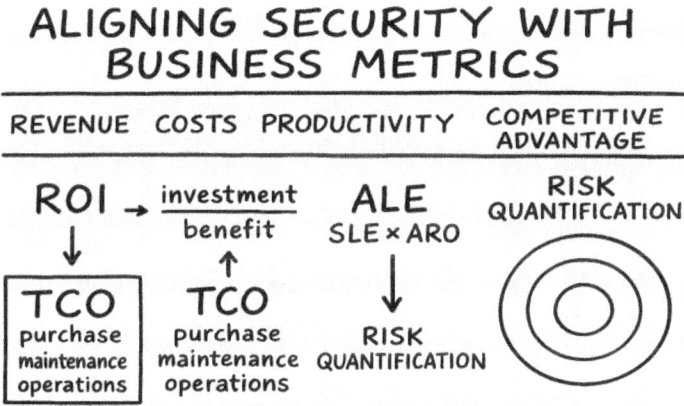

* * *

As the meeting wrapped up, Maya noticed a figure lingering by the doorway. Gerald Turner, the longest-serving security architect at TechForward, had been quietly observing the session. His salt-and-pepper beard reached halfway down his chest, and wire-rimmed glasses perched on his nose. The team had nicknamed him "The Oracle" for his uncanny ability to predict security incidents before they happened.

Gerald ambled over, his weathered hands clasping a mug that read "I survived Y2K and all I got was this lousy career in cybersecurity."

"Mind if I add something?" His voice was soft, yet it carried weight that commanded attention. The room fell silent.

"I've been in this game since we were worried about floppy disk viruses," Gerald said, leaning against the whiteboard. "I wrote my first security policy on WordPerfect. I've seen security teams treated like gods, pariahs, and everything in between."

Jessica leaned forward, captivated.

"What Maya's teaching you about business translation isn't just a tactic, it's survival." Gerald's eyes crinkled at the corners. "In the '90s, we were the wizards with arcane knowledge. In the 2000s, we became the Department of No. But today? Today we're either business partners or we're irrelevant."

He took a sip from his mug. "The teams I've seen fail weren't the ones with technical gaps. They were the ones who couldn't translate their value. They spoke security while the business spoke money. Different languages entirely."

Maya nodded, appreciating his perspective.

"The moment you start speaking business outcomes," Gerald continued, "something magical happens. You stop being the security person and start being a trusted advisor. Budgets appear. Priorities shift. People stop avoiding you in the hallway."

Jessica suppressed a laugh.

"I watched a brilliant CISO get fired because he couldn't explain why his multi-million dollar security program mattered in business terms. Meanwhile, I've seen junior analysts get promoted because they could tie every recommendation to revenue protection or competitive advantage."

Gerald straightened up. "This isn't just about getting what you want. It's about ensuring security actually happens. Because if they don't understand the business value, they won't prioritize it, no matter how right you are technically."

Jessica scribbled furiously in her notebook, goosebumps visible on her arms.

"Remember," Gerald said, his voice dropping to almost a whisper, "in the language of business, the most persuasive dialect is always ROI."

* * *

Maya caught Gerald's eye and nodded with quiet appreciation. His decades of experience had distilled wisdom that perfectly complemented her teaching.

"Trust," Gerald said, setting his mug down. "That's what we're really building here. Speaking their language gets you in the door, but reliability is what keeps you at the table."

Maya reflected on her own journey. How many times had delivering consistently, not just in crises but in everyday interactions, elevated her influence beyond her title?

"When you consistently translate security into business outcomes," Gerald continued, "you become the person they seek out before decisions, not after. You transform from a checkpoint to a compass."

Maya watched understanding bloom across her team's faces. This was the lesson she'd most wanted them to grasp.

"Humans are simple creatures at heart," Gerald concluded with a gentle smile. "We value those we can trust. Not just with our secrets, but with our goals. When you become trustworthy in their language, not yours, that's when security truly happens."

As the team filed out, Maya remained still, feeling the weight of Gerald's words settle into place like the final piece of a complex puzzle. Trust, after all, was the true currency of influence.

Chapter 5:

Build Trust Through

Consistency, Not Control

Maya arranged the conference room for Friday's intern session with the same care she always did. These weekly meetings were a highlight, a chance to nurture the next generation while keeping her own thinking fresh and current. She set out a small tray of pastries and brewed a pot of coffee, knowing the team would appreciate both after a long week.

Jessica arrived first, notebook in hand, her enthusiasm undiminished despite the grueling pace of her internship. The others filtered in gradually: Priya with her ever-present coffee mug, Malik scrolling through his phone, and Gerald, who rarely missed these sessions despite having no formal mentoring responsibilities.

"So," Maya began once everyone had settled, "any burning questions from the week?"

Jessica leaned forward. "Actually, yes. We've been talking about trust all week, and I'm curious, how do you actually build it? It seems like some securlty teams are feared, and others are valued. What makes the difference?"

Maya smiled, recognizing the perfect teaching moment. "That's an excellent question. Who wants to take a first crack at it?"

Priya set down her coffee. "Fear is easy. Trust is hard. I learned that lesson in the Army. My first SOC manager ruled through intimidation; people followed procedures because they were afraid not to. But the moment he wasn't looking..." She shrugged. "Shadow IT flourished. Problems went unreported. We were actually less secure because of it."

"Authority can force compliance," Gerald added, "but only consistency builds trust. People need to know you'll be the same person tomorrow that you were today."

Maya nodded. "That's key. Trust isn't built through grand gestures; it's built through small, consistent interactions. When you say you'll do something, do it. When you make a mistake, own it."

"And listen more than you talk," Malik chimed in. "When I moved from the red team to AppSec, I had to earn developers' trust. They'd been burned by security people who swooped in, dropped requirements, and disappeared. I started by asking questions instead of giving answers."

"That's exactly it," Maya said. "Trusted security teams aren't the ones with the most authority; they're the ones who show up consistently, speak honestly, and focus on enabling rather than blocking. They're partners, not police."

Jessica scribbled notes furiously. "So consistency, not authority..."

"And remember," Maya concluded, "trust is fragile. It takes months to build, seconds to break, and forever to repair. Guard it carefully."

* * *

Gerald shifted in his chair, the weathered leather of his boots creaking against the floor. His eyes had that distant look Maya recognized; he was about to drop wisdom that only came from decades in the trenches.

"Security is a unique discipline," Gerald began, stroking his salt-and-pepper beard. "Unlike accounting or engineering, we operate almost entirely in uncertainty. We don't know when the attack will occur, what form it will take, or whether our controls will be effective. We're essentially asking the organization to invest in protection against things they can't see, based on our word alone."

Maya nodded, watching Jessica's eyes widen slightly. This was the kind of perspective interns rarely heard.

"That uncertainty," Gerald continued, "is why trust isn't just nice to have, it's our operating system. Without it, we're just the department of 'no' with fancy tools."

Priya leaned forward. "I see this every day in the SOC. When teams trust us, they report anomalies immediately. When they don't, they hide things until it's too late."

"Exactly," Gerald said. "In uncertainty, people follow those they trust, not just those with the right title. I've seen brilliant security strategies fail because teams didn't trust the messenger. And I've seen basic security practices flourish under leaders who built genuine trust."

Maya watched the concept sink in around the table. "Trust becomes our currency," she added. "It determines whether people call us before they make decisions or after problems emerge."

Gerald nodded. "In my forty years, I've never seen a successful security program that wasn't built on trust. Think about it, we're asking developers to slow down, executives to spend money, and employees to change habits. Without trust, all we get is compliance theater, actions without commitment."

"So, how do you measure it?" Jessica asked. "Trust seems so... intangible."

"You measure it by what happens when you're not in the room," Gerald replied. "Are people making security decisions without being forced? Are they coming to you with problems before they escalate? Those are your trust metrics."

Maya smiled, grateful for Gerald's perspective. The Oracle had distilled decades of experience into something profound yet practical. Trust wasn't just about relationships; it was the foundation that made security possible in a world of unknowns.

* * *

Maya smiled gratefully at Gerald. "Thank you for that perspective. It reminds me of Jamie, my mentor at FinSecure." She leaned back in her chair, her eyes taking on that reflective quality her team had come to recognize.

"When I joined FinSecure, Jamie was known as 'The Hammer.' Every security review ended with a list of deficiencies and a deadline. Teams dreaded working with her, and they'd find creative ways to bypass security reviews entirely." Maya shook her head. "The compliance numbers looked great, but shadow IT was everywhere."

Priya nodded knowingly. "Classic security theater."

"Exactly," Maya continued. "Then the company got hit, a breach through a shadow system no one had disclosed to security. Jamie could have doubled down, created more rigid controls. Instead, she did something that changed my entire perspective on security leadership."

Jessica leaned forward, notebook ready. "What did she do?"

"She stopped enforcing standards and started helping teams succeed safely. She'd begin every conversation with 'What are you trying to accomplish?' instead of 'Here's what you're doing wrong.' She reframed her team as guides rather than gatekeepers."

Maya traced a pattern on the table with her finger. "Within six months, teams were voluntarily bringing their projects to security earlier. Shadow IT reports increased because people were no longer afraid to disclose them. Actual security posture improved while reported compliance metrics temporarily dropped."

"Because they were finally seeing the real picture," Gerald nodded.

"When I came to TechForward, I tried to bring that same approach," Maya said. "I told the team we weren't here to say no, we were here to find secure ways to say yes. Some embraced it immediately."

Her eyes flickered briefly toward Priya, who shifted uncomfortably.

"Others were skeptical," Maya continued. "They'd seen leaders talk about partnership while still measuring success by how many vulnerabilities they found or projects they blocked."

"It felt like abandoning our responsibility," Priya admitted. "If we're not enforcing standards, what are we even doing?"

Maya nodded. "That's the challenge. The results were mixed at first. Some teams responded immediately to our partnership approach. Others tested boundaries, thinking we'd gone soft."

"The Product team," Xander muttered.

"The turning point came with the Apex client portal launch," Maya said. "Remember how rushed that was? Instead of throwing up roadblocks, we embedded with the team. We helped them prioritize security work that mattered most for launch. We took on some of the implementation ourselves."

"And they actually listened," Priya acknowledged. "I was surprised."

"They listened because we weren't just pointing out problems, we were invested in their success," Maya said. "Since then, we've seen a forty percent increase in early security consultations. Not because we mandated it, but because teams see value in working with us."

Gerald's eyes crinkled with approval. "You shifted from being perceived as an obstacle to being recognized as a guide."

"We're still finding our balance," Maya admitted. "There are days when I question if we're being too accommodating, especially when deadlines loom. But I keep coming back to what Jamie taught me: Security without trust is just an illusion of safety."

Jessica was scribbling furiously in her notebook. "So trust isn't just about being nice. It's actually more effective."

Maya nodded. "Trust is the difference between teams that follow security practices because they have to and teams that follow them because they want to. And that difference matters most when no one's watching."

* * *

Jessica's pen stilled over her notebook. "But what about when things get complicated and security fails? How do we save face?"

Maya recognized the anxiety behind the question, the fear that haunted every security professional. She met Jessica's gaze directly, seeing not just the question but the opportunity it presented.

"That's exactly when trust matters most," she said. "The instinct to protect our reputation is powerful, but it's also dangerous."

Maya reached for her laptop and pulled up a slide from her incident response training. "When I first became a security lead at NetCore, we discovered a misconfiguration in our AWS environment. Nothing had been breached, but customer data had been potentially exposed for forty-eight hours."

The team leaned in, sensing this wasn't a story Maya told often.

"My first instinct was to fix it quietly and hope no one noticed. After all, there was no evidence of actual access." Maya's voice softened. "But my director taught me something I never forgot. He said, 'How we handle this moment will define trust in our team for years.'"

She closed her laptop. "We disclosed immediately to leadership, to affected teams, to customers. We didn't have all the answers yet. We couldn't promise it would never happen again. But we were transparent about what we knew, what we didn't know, and what we were doing."

"And how did that go over?" Jessica asked, her pen hovering.

"In the short term? It was uncomfortable. There were tough questions. Some people were angry." Maya's expression remained calm. "But something unexpected happened. Teams started coming to us with their own security concerns, knowing we wouldn't shoot the messenger. Leadership included us in strategic discussions earlier because they trusted our judgment."

Gerald nodded. "Dale Carnegie principle. Admitting mistakes disarms critics faster than any defense."

"Exactly," Maya said. "When you apologize early and take responsibility, you shift the conversation from blame to solutions. It's counterintuitive, but acknowledging failure builds more trust than projecting perfection."

Priya shifted in her seat. "But there are legal considerations. Disclosure timing matters."

"Absolutely," Maya agreed. "I'm not suggesting we broadcast vulnerabilities before they're patched or ignore legal counsel. But there's a difference between strategic timing and hiding information."

She drew a simple timeline on the whiteboard. "The trust equation changes depending on how information comes to light. If we disclose it, we maintain control of the narrative. If someone else discovers our failure, the damage multiplies."

Jessica frowned. "But doesn't admitting security failures make us look incompetent?"

"That depends on how we frame it," Maya said. "Security isn't the absence of incidents, it's how effectively we respond to them. Perfect security doesn't exist. Teams that pretend otherwise are either lying or don't know what they don't know."

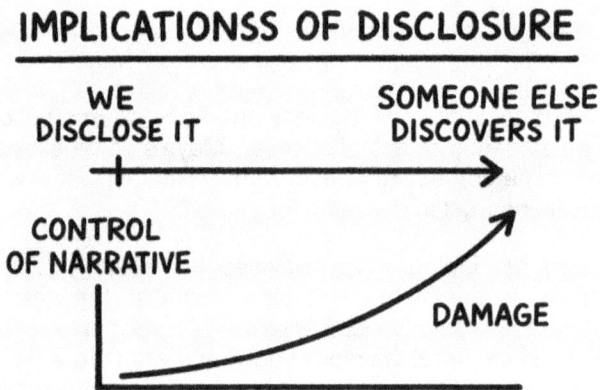

IMPLICATIONSS OF DISCLOSURE

WE DISCLOSE IT · **SOMEONE ELSE DISCOVERS IT**

CONTROL OF NARRATIVE

DAMAGE

She erased the whiteboard. "The most respected security teams I've worked with share their lessons learned. They say, 'Here's what happened, here's what we missed, here's how we're improving.' That transparency builds credibility."

Maya looked around the room, meeting each person's eyes. "Remember, we're not selling perfect security. We're building trust in our process, our expertise, and our integrity. Trust is resilient; it can survive failure. But it can't survive deception."

Jessica nodded slowly, understanding dawning in her expression. "So, it's better to be trusted than to look perfect."

"Every time," Maya said quietly. "Because when trust is gone, nothing else matters."

* * *

Gerald cleared his throat, tugging thoughtfully at his salt-and-pepper beard. "Reminds me of Catherine Voss at Meridian Systems back in the early 2000s."

Maya leaned forward, intrigued. Gerald rarely shared stories from his past.

"Catherine wasn't the most technically brilliant CISO I've worked with," Gerald continued, his weathered hands gesturing as if mapping the past in the air. "But she built the most effective security program I've ever seen through sheer reliability."

He smiled at the memory. "Every Monday, she published three security priorities for the week. Every Friday, she reported back on what had been done, what hadn't, and why. No excuses, just facts."

Maya noticed how the room had quieted, everyone drawn into Gerald's storytelling.

"During the big Blaster worm outbreak, while other companies were in chaos, Catherine had already patched our systems, not because she predicted it, but because she'd committed to regular patching cycles and never missed one. Not once in five years."

Gerald adjusted his glasses. "When she finally left, the CEO told me, 'I never understood half of what Catherine said about security, but I trusted her completely.' That's power you can't buy with budget or authority."

Priya nodded, a rare smile crossing her face. "Reminds me of Colonel Ellis in Army Cyber."

Maya watched as Priya straightened slightly, her posture always shifting when she referenced her military experience.

"Ellis wasn't warm or chatty. Honestly, terrified most junior analysts." Priya's eyes focused on something distant. "But he had this iron-clad reputation. If Ellis said something would happen, it happened. Period."

She tapped her pen against the table. "During a joint exercise, our systems detected anomalous traffic that looked like a breach. While other teams argued about jurisdiction and blame, Ellis simply said, 'My team will have answers in four hours.'"

"Four hours later, not three, not five, he delivered a complete assessment. No breach, but he'd found a previously unknown vulnerability. By the next morning, he had a patch ready."

Priya looked directly at Maya. "When I transferred to his command, he told me something I never forgot: 'In security, your word is your weapon. Don't promise what you can't deliver and never fail to deliver what you promise.'"

Maya nodded, seeing how these stories resonated with everyone in the room. Trust wasn't abstract; it was built through countless small moments of follow-through that, over time, became an unshakable foundation.

* * *

Maya noticed the heavy silence that had settled over the conference room. The weight of Gerald and Priya's stories hung in the air, creating a moment of collective reflection that felt almost sacred. But she also recognized the glazed look beginning to form in Jessica's eyes and the subtle shift in postures around the table.

"And on that inspirational note," Maya said with a warm smile, "I'd like to remind everyone that it's Friday, we've been at this for almost two hours, and there are still those chocolate chip cookies from Rebecca's birthday that no one's touched." She gestured toward the snack table. "Security might run on trust, but humans run on sugar."

The tension broke as people chuckled, stretching in their seats. Xander made an immediate beeline for the cookies, mumbling something about "strategic caloric reserves."

Maya watched as the team relaxed, then tapped her notebook. "Before we break, I want to pull this conversation back to something practical. We've heard powerful stories about trust-building, but how do we actually implement this in our daily work?"

She stood and walked to the whiteboard, marker in hand. "I've found there are four concrete practices that build trust faster than anything else."

Maya wrote as she spoke: "First, make commitments you know you can keep. This sounds obvious, but it's where most of us fail. We want to be helpful, so we overpromise." She circled the word 'commitments.' "Better to promise less and deliver more than the reverse."

Priya nodded, her usual skepticism softened. "In the SOC, we started giving time ranges instead of deadlines. 'Between three and five hours' gives us room to be thorough while setting clear expectations."

"Exactly," Maya said, writing 'realistic timeframes' on the board. "Second practice: proactive communication. Don't wait to be asked for updates."

Malik raised his hand. "This was huge for my team. We set up automated status pages for our security reviews. Even when we're behind, teams appreciate knowing where they stand."

"That's brilliant," Maya said. "The third practice is something I call 'surprise elimination.' In security, surprises are almost always negative. Each time you eliminate a surprise, by flagging an issue early or preventing an unexpected roadblock, you make a deposit in the trust bank."

She paused, looking around the room. "And finally, acknowledge mistakes quickly. Nothing, and I mean nothing, builds trust faster than saying 'I was wrong' or 'we missed this.'"

Jessica, the intern, looked troubled. "But doesn't admitting mistakes make people trust us less?"

Maya smiled. "Great question. Actually, research shows the opposite. Vulnerability, when paired with competence, deepens trust. People don't expect perfection, they expect honesty."

She capped her marker. "These aren't just nice ideas. They're practical tools that transform how others see us. Remember, in security, we're asking people to follow our guidance on things they often can't see or fully understand. That requires extraordinary trust."

Maya glanced at Gerald, who gave an approving nod. "As our stories today showed, trust isn't built in crisis moments, it's built in countless small interactions where we prove ourselves reliable, transparent, and human."

The team began gathering their belongings, and conversation flowed more naturally now. Maya watched them, knowing that Monday would bring new challenges, but feeling confident that the seeds planted today would grow into something lasting.

PRACTICES THAT BUILD TRUST

- ## MAKE COMMITMENTS YOU CAN KEEP
  ### REALISTIC TIMEFRAMES

- ## PROACTIVE COMMUNICATION

- ## SURPRISE ELIMINATION

- ## ACKNOWLEDGE MISTAKES QUICKLY

* * *

Maya gathered her laptop and notebook, nodding to team members as they filed out of the conference room. She noticed Jessica lingering by the door, clearly waiting for an opportunity to speak. The intern's expression was thoughtful, her usual energy tempered by reflection.

"Something on your mind, Jessica?" Maya asked, sliding her laptop into her bag.

Jessica stepped forward. "I've been thinking about everything we discussed today. I want to make sure I understand it correctly." She hesitated, then continued with growing confidence. "It seems like what you're saying is that trust isn't built through grand gestures or perfect security policies, it's built through all these tiny moments where we prove ourselves reliable."

Maya nodded encouragingly. "Go on."

"So when I commit to reviewing a developer's code by Thursday, and I actually do it on Wednesday with helpful comments, that's a trust deposit,"

Jessica said. "And when I admit I don't know something instead of faking it, that's another deposit. It's like we're building this... this invisible account with everyone we work with."

"That's exactly right," Maya said, impressed by the intern's insight.

"And it's not just about being nice," Jessica continued, her eyes brightening with understanding. "It's strategic. Because later, when we need to influence decisions or get support for security initiatives, people remember all those small moments. They think, 'Jessica always delivers what she promises' or 'Maya always gives me the straight story, even when it's tough.'"

Maya leaned against the doorframe. "You've captured it perfectly. Trust is the foundation of influence. Without it, we're just another voice making demands."

Jessica nodded eagerly. "And what struck me most was that consistency matters more than being right. Like, we could have the perfect technical solution, but if people don't trust us, they won't implement it anyway."

"Which makes all our technical expertise worthless," Maya finished.

"It's funny," Jessica said with a small laugh. "In my classes, we spent so much time on tools and techniques, but almost nothing on how to build the trust needed to actually get people to use them."

Maya smiled. "That's why you're here, to learn what they don't teach in classrooms."

As they walked toward the elevator, Jessica added, "I think I understand now why you meet with Product every week, even when there's nothing urgent to discuss. You're not just checking boxes, you're building that trust account for when you really need it."

"Smart observation," Maya said, feeling a quiet pride in Jessica's growth. "Trust is the currency of influence. And like any currency, you have to earn it before you can spend it."

* * *

Maya pressed the elevator button, a thoughtful expression crossing her face. The teaching moment wasn't quite complete.

"Jessica, you've grasped something essential that took me years to learn," she said. "Trust absolutely gives us a voice at the table. But there's another level beyond that I want you to consider."

Jessica tilted her head, curiosity evident. "What's that?"

"Think about the difference between people trusting your security advice and people feeling ownership of security themselves." Maya watched as understanding begn to dawn in Jessica's eyes. "When security becomes their idea rather than ours, that's when we get real momentum."

The elevator arrived with a soft chime. As they stepped in, Maya continued, "The most powerful moment in security isn't when someone implements your recommendation, it's when they come to you excited about a security improvement they thought of themselves."

Jessica nodded slowly, processing this.

"Ponder that over the weekend," Maya said with a small smile as the elevator reached the lobby. "How might we move from being trusted advisors to being catalysts for others' ownership? That's where sustainable security culture begins."

Jessica's expression told Maya the seed had been planted. Perfect timing for next week's discussions.

Chapter 6:

Make Security Their Idea,

Not Your Mandate

Maya watched the elevator doors close as Jessica disappeared from view. The conversation lingered in her mind, triggering a memory from three years ago.

The conference room had been empty except for Maya and the peculiar man sitting across from her. He'd introduced himself simply as "Callahan," though everyone at the firm called him "the Gray Hat." The VC partners had sent him to mentor her after her promotion to Deputy Director of Security.

"So your team is refusing to implement the new access controls," he'd said, not as a question but a statement of fact. His voice was soft, almost melodic, but it carried weight.

Maya had nodded, frustration evident. "I've shown them the data. I've explained the risks. I've cited industry standards. They just... resist."

The Gray Hat had placed his weathered Moleskine notebook on the table, open to a blank page. "Tell me about your last successful security initiative. One where people actually embraced the change."

She'd thought for a moment. "The API authentication overhaul. It went surprisingly well."

"What was different about that one?"

"I'm not sure. The engineering leads were on board from day one. They even started suggesting improvements to my original design."

He'd smiled then, the corners of his eyes crinkling. "And how did that project begin?"

The realization had hit her. "I didn't present it as a finished solution. I brought the problem statement to their architecture meeting and asked for input."

The Gray Hat had written something in his notebook. "People resist what's imposed but defend what they help create."

That principle had transformed Maya's approach. She'd learned that security mandates, no matter how logical or necessary, faced an uphill battle against human psychology. But security ideas that emerged collaboratively, where teams felt genuine ownership, gained momentum almost effortlessly.

After that meeting, she went back to her resistant team with a different approach. Instead of presenting her solution, she'd shared the problem and invited their expertise. The resulting security framework wasn't exactly what she'd originally envisioned, but it was better. And more importantly, it was implemented without the usual friction.

Maya smiled at the memory as she walked through the company lobby. The Gray Hat had appeared at precisely the right moment in her career, when she'd been skilled enough to be dangerous but not yet wise enough to be effective. His counsel had accelerated her growth beyond technical expertise into true leadership.

She'd never forget the day he'd shown up to their final mentoring session wearing a pink unicorn onesie, completely straight-faced, to make a point about "pattern interruption" in security awareness. The memory still made her laugh.

His methods had been unorthodox, but the results spoke for themselves. Within a year of those sessions, security incidents had decreased by 30%, while team satisfaction scores had risen dramatically. The principles he'd taught her about human psychology and organizational change had proven more valuable than any technical certification.

As Maya pushed through the revolving door into the crisp evening air, she made a mental note to incorporate this principle into next week's strategy session. Jessica showed promise, the kind Maya had once shown before the Gray Hat's guidance.

Maya pulled out her phone, scrolling to a note she'd made years ago: "Mandated security creates compliance at best. Co-created security builds a culture of defense."

The wisdom was as relevant now as it had been then. Perhaps it was time to pass along not just what she knew, but how she'd learned it.

* * *

Maya spotted Jessica waiting at their usual corner table in the company café. She'd been looking forward to this lunch all morning, especially after spending her entire weekend engaged in hand-to-hand combat with the stubborn dandelions that had staged a hostile takeover of her garden beds.

"Sorry, I'm a coupleof minutes late," Maya said, setting down her tray. "Budget meeting ran long."

Jessica looked up from her phone with a bright smile. "No problem. I was just scrolling through apartment decorating ideas. Still can't believe I have my own place now."

"How's the new apartment working out?" Maya asked, genuinely curious. There was something refreshing about Jessica's enthusiasm that made Maya feel both nostalgic and energized.

"It's amazing! I mean, it's tiny and the kitchen is basically a closet with a microwave, but it's mine. No more roommates leaving passive-aggressive notes about milk or playing EDM at three in the morning." Jessica's eyes lit up. "I actually sat in complete silence for an hour on Saturday just because I could."

Maya laughed. "That sounds like heaven. My weekend was less peaceful. I decided to wage war on the weeds in my garden." She rubbed her lower back unconsciously. "My body keeps finding creative new ways to remind me I'm not in college anymore."

"Garden troubles?" Jessica asked between bites of her sandwich.

"Let's just say I discovered muscles I didn't know existed. There's apparently a very specific 'pulling weeds' muscle group that only activates after thirty-five." Maya winced dramatically. "How did I once dance until sunrise and now feel betrayed by my body after two hours of gardening?"

They shared a laugh, and Maya steered the conversation toward work. She wanted to introduce the concept of ownership without making it feel like a lecture.

"So, how's the access control project coming along? The one the dev team was pushing back on?"

Jessica's expression clouded. "Honestly? Not great. I sent them the implementation plan with all the security requirements, and they basically ghosted me. Derek finally responded yesterday, saying they 'need to prioritize feature work' right now."

Maya nodded thoughtfully. "Sounds familiar. Mind if I ask how you approached it with them?"

"I did everything by the book," Jessica said, frustration evident. "I documented the compliance requirements, outlined the security benefits, and even included case studies of breaches that happened without proper access controls."

"And still nothing?"

"Radio silence. I don't get it, the solution is so obviously necessary."

Maya took a sip of her water. "What if I told you the approach might matter more than the solution itself?"

Jessica looked puzzled. "What do you mean?"

"Let me ask you something. Remember when you moved into your apartment, did you immediately know exactly how you wanted to arrange everything?"

"Not really. I've been moving furniture around almost daily, trying different layouts."

"And if your landlord had dictated exactly where each piece had to go?"

Jessica wrinkled her nose. "I'd hate that. It's my space. I want to decide how it works."

Maya smiled. "That's exactly how dev teams feel about their code."

Understanding dawned on Jessica's face. "So instead of presenting a complete solution..."

"What might happen if you brought them the problem instead?" Maya suggested.

Jessica set down her fork, clearly processing. "So rather than saying 'implement these controls,' I could ask how they'd solve the access management risks?"

"Exactly. People resist what's imposed but defend what they help create."

"That makes so much sense," Jessica said, her eyes widening. "It's not about watering down the security requirements, it's about how they're introduced."

Maya nodded. "Security solutions that teams help design almost always get implemented faster and with fewer exceptions than mandates from on high."

"I think I've been approaching this all wrong," Jessica said, pulling out her notebook. "What if I scheduled a working session instead of sending requirements? Let them help design the solution?"

Maya smiled, watching Jessica work through the concept on her own. "That sounds like an excellent approach. What might that look like specifically?"

As Jessica began sketching out a new plan, Maya felt a quiet satisfaction. The seed was planted, and Jessica was already making it her own idea.

* * *

Maya gathered her notes and headed toward the elevator, mentally rehearsing key points for the marketing meeting. Lost in thought, she didn't notice Amira until the communications director fell into step beside her.

"That was quite the Jedi mind trick I just witnessed," Amira said with a sly smile. "Teaching Jessica about ownership by making her own the concept of ownership. Very meta."

Maya laughed, surprised. "Were you eavesdropping on my lunch?"

"Not intentionally. I was grabbing coffee when you two sat down." Amira pressed the elevator button. "But I couldn't help noticing your approach. You never once told her what to do, just asked questions until she figured it out herself."

The elevator doors opened, and they stepped inside.

"I had an uncle like that growing up," Maya said, leaning against the wall. "Most annoying man alive. Every conversation was just questions. 'What do you think about that, Maya?' 'How might that work?' 'What other approaches could you try?'" She mimicked his deep voice. "Never a straight answer, just endless Socratic dialogue."

"Sounds maddening," Amira said.

"It was! I'd ask him something simple like whether I should join the debate club, and he'd launch into twenty questions about my interests and goals instead of just giving advice."

The elevator stopped at the third floor, but no one got on.

"It wasn't until my thirties that I really got it," Maya continued. "I picked up philosophy as a hobby, classic millennial, finding my moral framework in middle age after the world fell apart a few times."

"As one does," Amira nodded with a knowing smile.

74

"I was reading Plato's Republic, and suddenly my uncle's approach clicked. Socrates never lectured. He just asked questions that led people to their own realizations." Maya adjusted her laptop bag. "But the real epiphany came from watching this guy at my daughter's school PTA."

"PTA? That's where you found philosophical enlightenment?"

"Oddly enough. There was a dad, Mike, who somehow managed to get everyone doing all the work while they thanked him for the opportunity. The weird part was, everyone loved him."

The elevator doors opened on their floor, and they stepped out.

"What was his secret?" Amira asked.

"He never told anyone what to do. He just asked questions. 'What if we tried this?' 'How would that work?' Sound familiar? People would walk away feeling like they'd come up with brilliant ideas themselves, when they were actually doing exactly what he wanted."

They paused outside the conference room where the marketing team was gathering.

"And that's when it all clicked for me," Maya said. "Influence isn't about making declarations or showing how smart you are. It's about helping others discover solutions in a way that gives them ownership."

Amira nodded thoughtfully. "So instead of telling Jessica how to approach the dev team..."

"I just helped her realize there was a better way. Now she's not implementing my solution, she's championing her own." Maya smiled. "And she'll fight ten times harder for it because it feels like hers."

"Very clever," Amira said. "I might need to borrow that approach with my communications team."

"Be my guest. Just don't tell them I told you to do it," Maya winked as they entered the conference room. "Let them think it was your idea all along."

"Even better," Amira replied. "I'll make them think it's their idea."

"Touché!"

* * *

Maya and Amira exited the marketing meeting, with Amira still contemplating their earlier conversation. As they headed toward the quarterly sales review, Amira gestured toward the coffee shop in the lobby.

"I need caffeine before we face the Q3 projections. Join me?"

Maya checked her watch. "We've got fifteen minutes. Cold brew sounds perfect."

As they waited for their drinks, Amira leaned against the counter. "I can't stop thinking about what you said earlier. This ownership concept, have you seen it work on a larger scale? Beyond one-on-one mentoring?"

Maya smiled, collecting her drink. "Actually, yes. At FinSecure, before I joined TechForward, we had an annual security review that everyone dreaded. Three days of mandatory meetings where security teams would basically lecture product teams about all their failings."

"Sounds delightful," Amira said dryly.

"Oh, it was brutal. Attendance was technically required, but people would suddenly develop mysterious illnesses or urgent client calls." Maya stirred her cold brew. "Then Jamie, our AppSec lead, had this idea. Instead of calling it a 'security review,' he reframed it as a 'product resilience workshop.'"

"Clever rebrand," Amira noted as they walked toward the elevator.

"It was more than that. He completely flipped the format. Instead of security presenting problems, product teams presented their roadmaps first. Then everyone, developers, product managers, security folks, worked together to identify potential risks and solutions."

"And people actually showed up for this?"

Maya nodded. "Not just showed up, they participated. Jamie structured it so that teams would break into small groups with mixed expertise. He'd pose questions like, 'If you wanted to compromise this feature, how would you do it?' Suddenly, everyone was thinking like an attacker."

"That's brilliant," Amira said. "Turn it into a game."

"Exactly. By the second day, people were coming up with solutions before security could even identify all the problems. One product manager told me it was the first time she felt like security was actually trying to help her succeed rather than just pointing out flaws."

The elevator doors opened on the executive floor.

"The real magic happened on the final day," Maya continued. "Teams presented their own security plans. Not security telling them what to do, but them telling us what they were going to do. And they were passionate about it because they'd developed the solutions themselves."

"And the follow-through?" Amira asked.

"That's the best part. Implementation rates jumped from about 40% to over 85%. People defended these solutions in their sprint planning meetings. When the next workshop came around, teams were actually disappointed when scheduling conflicts meant it had to be shortened."

"From dreaded obligation to disappointed it's ending," Amira mused. "That's quite a transformation."

"That's the power of ownership," Maya said as they reached the conference room. "People fight for their own ideas in ways they never will for someone else's mandates."

* * *

Amira stopped just outside the conference room door, a slow smile spreading across her face. "Wait a minute. Have you played this game on us, here at TechForward?"

Maya took a sip of her cold brew, her eyes crinkling slightly above the rim of her cup. Of course, she had. Once you knew the trick, you used it everywhere, especially in a new organization where you needed to build credibility fast.

"What makes you think that?" Maya asked innocently.

"The data privacy framework. The one that came out of that chaotic all-hands last quarter." Amira narrowed her eyes. "You barely spoke during that meeting, just asked questions. Then somehow we all walked out feeling like we'd collectively invented something brilliant."

Maya shrugged, not confirming or denying. The truth was, she'd been planting seeds for weeks before that meeting, having coffee chats with key stakeholders, asking pointed questions about their privacy concerns, listening carefully to their frustrations.

"My favorite success story wasn't here, though," Maya said, changing the subject. "It was Fred Donovan at my previous company. Just retired last year."

"Fred?"

"Great guy, brilliant engineer, but he was... set in his ways. Fifty years of coding experience, which meant fifty years of causing security flaws in applications."

Amira leaned against the wall, intrigued. "The old guard, huh?"

"He'd ramble on about telephone switches controlling model trains in a leaky WWII building back in college. His security philosophy was basically: if everything is open, nothing needs protection." Maya shook her head, remembering. "Getting Fred to care about security was like trying to convince a cat to take swimming lessons."

"So what did you do?"

"For months, he excluded my team from his project's planning meetings. Said we'd just slow things down." Maya checked her watch; five minutes until the meeting. "Then I noticed how much he loved mentoring junior engineers. So I started sending them to him with security questions, pretending I was stumped."

"You didn't."

"I did. 'Fred, this encryption approach seems elegant, but I can't figure out why it's failing these tests.' He'd solve it, then explain to them why security mattered in that specific context."

"Sneaky," Amira said with approval.

"After a few weeks, I invited him to guest lecture at our security brown bag lunch. Not to learn, to teach. By the time he finished explaining buffer overflows to a room full of developers, he was correcting his own past mistakes."

"And he never caught on?"

Maya smiled. "Maybe he did, eventually. However, by then, he had already become our most vocal security advocate. Started demanding security reviews for his own code. Even created this little checklist that all the senior engineers started using."

"Turning Fred into a security advocate, that's impressive."

"In my mind, it's the greatest success of my career," Maya admitted. "It felt like I'd taken out the Emperor and destroyed the Death Star all at the same time."

"Because he influenced others?"

"Exactly. When Fred started talking about secure coding practices, people who'd ignored me for months suddenly became interested. He had credibility I couldn't match."

Amira checked her phone as a notification appeared. "Two-minute warning for the meeting."

"The funny part is, six months later, Fred took me aside and said, 'You know, I've been thinking about security all wrong my entire career.' As if he'd come to this revelation entirely on his own." Maya smiled at the memory. "And in a way, he had."

They pushed open the conference room door, where executives were already gathering for the quarterly review.

"So that's the real trick," Amira whispered. "Not just making it their idea, but making them forget it wasn't always their idea."

"Precisely," Maya said. "The best security influence is the kind no one realizes they're under."

* * *

The executive meeting concluded with a round of applause for the product team. Maya hung back as people filtered out, gathering her tablet and notes while exchanging brief pleasantries with the CTO. She felt a presence lingering behind her and turned to find Amira waiting, arms crossed, expression thoughtful.

"That was masterful," Amira said once they were alone. "I saw it the whole time."

Maya raised an eyebrow. "Saw what exactly?"

"You. Doing it again." Amira gestured vaguely. "The VP of Engineering just volunteered to implement that entire authentication framework you've been pushing for months. But you never actually suggested it, you just asked if he'd considered the implications of the current system during an acquisition."

Maya tucked her tablet under her arm. "He came to the right conclusion."

"And then you made sure everyone heard you say how brilliant his insight was." Amira shook her head in wonder. "One minute I'm watching this elegant cybersecurity professional in her perfect blazer, and the next I'm seeing... I don't know, some ancient Greek philosopher leading students to their own conclusions."

Maya laughed. "Socrates? I'll take that as a compliment, though I'm hoping to keep my hair and avoid the hemlock."

"Seriously, what's in that cold brew?" Amira nodded toward Maya's empty cup. "Because I need some. You've got executives practically falling over themselves to implement security measures they would have fought tooth and nail if you'd mandated them."

Maya checked the time. "I should head out, "

"No way." Amira blocked the doorway. "It's Friday, and I'm not letting you leave until you share some secrets. This isn't just about security, is it? This is a whole... philosophy."

Maya considered this, then set her bag down. "Fine. But I'm not giving away all my tricks."

"Just the good ones," Amira pressed.

"It's psychological ownership," Maya explained, leaning against the conference table. "People protect what they feel belongs to them. There's actual research on this: when people invest their ideas, time, or identity into something, they value it more highly."

"So, how do you create that?"

"Early involvement is key. Bring people in before decisions are made, not after. Ask questions that lead them to discover the problems themselves." Maya counted off on her fingers. "Give them control over how solutions are implemented. Publicly attribute ideas to them, even when they're building on your suggestions."

Amira's eyes widened. "That's why you're always saying 'as Kevin pointed out last week' even when Kevin definitely did not point that out."

"Maybe Kevin mentioned something tangentially related," Maya smiled. "The point is, Kevin now feels ownership of that idea, and he'll defend it."

"This isn't just security wisdom, is it?"

"No. It's in all those books you probably have on your shelf. Carnegie's 'How to Win Friends,' Voss's 'Never Split the Difference,' and even 'Thinking, Fast and Slow.' It's basic human psychology, we value what we create more than what others impose on us."

Amira looked thoughtful. "So when you stepped back during that privacy framework discussion..."

"I'd already had one-on-ones with most of the key players. I knew what they cared about, what worried them. During the meeting, I just connected the dots they were already drawing."

"And let them take credit."

"Credit is cheap compared to results," Maya said. "My job isn't to be right, it's to make us secure. If that means letting others feel like the heroes, I'm fine with that."

"The invisible hand of security," Amira mused.

"Something like that." Maya gathered her things. "The real trick is patience. You can't rush psychological ownership. You plant seeds and wait for them to grow."

"And meanwhile, you're just sitting back, asking innocent questions."

Maya smiled. "There's nothing innocent about my questions, Amira. They're the most powerful tools I have."

* * *

Maya watched with quiet amusement as Amira slipped into the back of yet another security architecture review. This marked the fifth meeting in three weeks at which the communications lead had appeared without a clear reason for attending. The pattern was becoming obvious to everyone except, perhaps, Amira herself.

"Since we're discussing external API security, I thought Communications should have visibility," Amira explained when the engineering director raised an eyebrow at her presence.

Maya suppressed a smile. The meeting wasn't remotely relevant to Amira's department, but she'd developed an almost scholarly interest in Maya's methods. What had begun as professional curiosity had evolved into something approaching obsession.

During the session, Maya noticed how Amira took detailed notes whenever she asked one of her carefully crafted questions, the kind that led developers to their own security revelations without Maya having to dictate solutions. When the lead engineer proudly announced his team would implement certificate pinning "as a proactive measure," Amira's eyes darted to Maya with knowing recognition.

After the meeting, Maya found a message waiting on her phone.

Did you see how he thought it was his idea? You never even mentioned certificate pinning! - A

Maya typed back: He came to the right conclusion. That's what matters.

The following day, Maya spotted Amira and Jessica huddled together in the company café. The security intern and the communications director made an unlikely pair, but they were deep in conversation, Jessica gesturing animatedly while Amira nodded, occasionally jotting something in her notebook.

"Should we be concerned about that alliance?" Maya's deputy director asked, following her gaze.

Maya shook her head. "I think it's exactly what we want."

Over the next few weeks, the pattern continued. Amira found reasons to attend security reviews. Jessica started asking increasingly nuanced questions during team meetings, questions that sounded suspiciously like Maya's own approach. Neither of them directly acknowledged what they were doing, but Maya recognized her own techniques being studied, dissected, and tentatively deployed.

On a Wednesday in mid-July, Maya received a calendar invitation: "Summer Intern Leadership Showcase." Jessica had been selected to present her key learnings to the executive team. Maya accepted immediately.

The boardroom was packed when Maya arrived. Jessica stood at the front, poised and professional in a blazer that looked newly purchased for the occasion. Amira sat in the front row, practically vibrating with anticipation.

"For my summer project," Jessica began, "I studied how security initiatives succeed or fail across organizations." She clicked to her first slide: "Psychological Ownership: The Hidden Key to Security Adoption."

Maya settled back in her chair, curious to see where this would go.

Jessica continued with remarkable confidence. "What I discovered is that security measures implemented as mandates typically see 30% adoption, while those where stakeholders feel ownership reach 86% adoption and sustainability."

The CEO leaned forward. "That's significant. How did you measure this?"

"I compared historical security initiatives here and interviewed teams about their experiences," Jessica explained. "The difference wasn't in the quality of the security controls, but in how they were introduced."

Jessica clicked to her next slide, which outlined a methodology that Maya recognized immediately, it was her own approach, systematized and named. "The Ownership Acceleration Framework," Jessica called it.

"When people discover security solutions themselves, they defend them fiercely," Jessica concluded. "This isn't about manipulation, it's about alignment. We create space for people to connect security with what they already value."

As the executives nodded appreciatively, Maya caught Amira's eye. The communications director gave her a small, knowing smile that said everything: Yes, we figured you out. And yes, we know you let us.

After the presentation, the CTO clapped Jessica on the shoulder. "Impressive insights for an intern. Where did you develop this framework?"

Jessica hesitated for just a moment. "I observed it in action here and then researched the psychological principles behind it."

She didn't mention Maya once. And somehow, that felt like the greatest success of all.

* * *

As the executives filtered out, Maya lingered in the boardroom, watching Jessica field questions with growing confidence. Something about the moment transported her back to a conversation with The Gray Hat three years earlier.

"The most powerful ideas are the ones people think they came up with themselves," he'd told her, perched on the edge of her desk in that ridiculous pink unicorn onesie he sometimes wore to "disarm corporate defense mechanisms."

"But isn't that manipulative?" she'd asked.

The Gray Hat had shaken his head. "Only if your goal is control. But if your goal is better security? You're just removing your ego from the equation."

Now, as Jessica explained the framework, Maya's framework, she felt a surprising tightness in her throat. She'd spent years perfecting this approach, and here it was, taking on a life beyond her. Knowledge flowing downstream, evolving, improving.

Jessica caught her eye across the room and gave a small nod of acknowledgment. Maya returned it with a smile that contained more emotion than she'd intended to reveal.

Later, alone in her office, Maya stared out the window at the summer afternoon. The organization had changed. Security wasn't her department anymore; it belonged to everyone. The cultural shift was undeniable.

"So, what now?" she whispered to herself.

She'd accomplished what she'd set out to do here. The foundations were solid. The next generation, people like Jessica, were carrying the work forward. Did she want to stay and nurture what she'd built, or was it time to find another broken system that needed fixing?

There was something appealing about starting fresh somewhere else. The challenge of it. The opportunity to fail in new and interesting ways. She smiled at the thought; failure had become less terrifying over the years.

Maya pulled out her phone and scrolled through her contacts until she found The Gray Hat's number. When was the last time they'd spoken? Six months ago? Longer?

She wondered what he was up to these days. Probably terrorizing some other security leader with his cryptic koans and uncomfortably penetrating questions.

Her finger hovered over the call button. Maybe it was time to reconnect. After all, the best mentors knew when their students needed a nudge toward the next challenge.

Chapter 7:

Collaborate on Solutions, Don't Dictate Requirements

Maya's phone buzzed on her nightstand at 5:04 AM, jolting her from sleep. The text was brief: "Leadership meeting. 7 AM. Boardroom. Critical." From Elena.

Thirty minutes later, showered and dressed in a charcoal suit she reserved for board presentations, Maya grabbed coffee from the empty break room. The office felt eerily quiet this early.

She wasn't the first to arrive. Elena was already there, looking uncharacteristically tense. Marc from Finance. Anika from Legal. And a figure that made Maya nearly drop her coffee, The Gray Hat, lounging at the far end of the table in a perfectly tailored suit instead of his usual casual attire.

He caught her eye and gave an almost imperceptible nod. Maya returned it with a subtle glare that promised retribution.

More executives filtered in. When the room was full, Elena stood.

"I'll keep this brief. A venture capital firm called Keystone Partners has approached our board with an acquisition offer." She gestured toward The Gray Hat. "Mr. Callahan represents their interests and will explain the details."

Maya's grip tightened around her coffee cup. So that's why he was here. Not as her mentor but as... what? The enemy? An opportunist?

The Gray Hat rose smoothly. "Keystone has been tracking TechForward's performance metrics for some time. Your latest client portal deployment at Apex demonstrated exactly what we've been looking for, security that enables business rather than constrains it."

For the next twenty minutes, he outlined Keystone's vision, their valuation of TechForward, and the proposed transition plan. Throughout, Maya caught him glancing her way, reading her reaction. She kept her face neutral despite the storm brewing inside.

When the meeting concluded, The Gray Hat approached. "Walk with me?"

"Not here," Maya replied, voice clipped.

"Of course not. Meet me at Riverside Park in an hour. The snow cone stand near the east entrance."

* * *

Maya found him sitting on a bench, holding two paper cups of shaved ice doused in colorful syrup. He handed her the blue one.

"You could have warned me," she said, accepting the snow cone.

"Would that have changed anything?"

"It would have given me time to process before sitting in a room full of people trying not to look shocked."

He nodded. "Fair point."

They walked in silence along the river path. Early morning joggers passed them. A family with small children fed ducks at the water's edge.

"So you're working for Keystone now?" Maya finally asked.

"Consulting. They asked for my assessment of TechForward's security posture and culture."

"And you told them to buy us."

"I told them you've built something remarkable." His eyes met hers. "Something worth investing in."

Maya took a bite of her snow cone, the cold momentarily numbing her tongue. "Why didn't you tell me you were evaluating us?"

"Would you have behaved differently if you knew?"

"No, but, "

"Exactly. That's what makes what you've built authentic."

They walked further, the city skyline visible through the trees.

"After this merger," The Gray Hat said, "the new organization will need comprehensive security policies. Wouldn't you agree?"

Maya frowned. "Of course."

"And what would be the best approach to creating those policies?"

She recognized his teaching mode activating. "You tell me."

"Will you be effective creating them all alone?"

The question hung in the air. Maya thought about the past year, the coalitions she'd built, the ownership she'd fostered, and the collaborative approach that had transformed their security culture.

"No," she admitted. "I won't."

"Why not?"

"Because policies created in isolation become shelfware. They need to reflect the reality of how work happens, not how I think it should happen."

The Gray Hat smiled. "And how will you ensure that happens in this new, larger organization?"

Maya paused, watching a leaf float down the river. "By bringing people into the process. Making them co-creators, not just recipients."

"Even when it would be faster to write them yourself?"

"Especially then." Maya felt the pieces clicking together. "This isn't just about the merger, is it? This is the next evolution of what we've been building."

The Gray Hat shrugged. "You tell me."

Maya looked out at the river, understanding dawning. "Security isn't something you impose. It's something you cultivate, together."

* * *

Maya leaned against the conference room wall, watching her team filter in. Faces she'd handpicked, shaped, and grown to trust. Now they were looking to her for certainty in uncertain times.

"Everyone settled?" she asked once the room quieted. "Good. Let's talk about what we know and what we don't."

She moved to the whiteboard and drew a simple line down the middle.

"We know Keystone values our security approach. We don't know exactly what the merged organization will look like." She wrote these points in their respective columns. "What else?"

Darius raised his hand. "We know our current policies work for us. We don't know if they'll work at scale."

Maya nodded, adding his points. "Excellent."

Lena, their newest analyst, spoke next. "We know our team has skills. We don't know if there will be... redundancies." The word hung heavy in the air.

Maya put down her marker and faced them directly. "I want to address that head-on. Yes, acquisitions often mean reorganization. I cannot promise that everyone's role will remain the same. What I can promise is that I'll fight for this team, and I'll support each of you whether you're part of the new organization or not."

She watched shoulders relax slightly.

"But that's exactly why we need to talk about the difference between compliance and commitment." Maya moved to the center of the room. "Keystone didn't acquire us because we check boxes. They acquired us because we built something that works."

She tapped the table. "What's the difference between compliance and commitment?"

"Compliance is doing what you're told," offered Raj. "Commitment is believing in why you're doing it."

"Exactly," Maya said. "And when people are just complying, what happens when no one's watching?"

"Corners get cut," several voices answered in unison.

"Which is why whatever we build next needs to be created collaboratively." Maya pulled up a slide showing a policy development framework. "This is what I'm proposing we do differently."

The team leaned forward as Maya explained her vision, cross-functional working groups, stakeholder interviews, and pilot implementations with feedback loops.

"But that will take forever," Lena objected. "Wouldn't it be faster if we just drafted everything ourselves?"

Maya smiled, remembering her conversation with The Gray Hat. "Faster? Yes. Better? No. When we collaborate, we surface hidden insights.

We discover the gaps between how work is supposed to happen and how it actually happens."

She thought about The Gray Hat's cryptic evaluation of her work. Was she honored? Unsettled? Maybe both. But his methods had pushed her to this realization.

"Here's what I've learned," Maya continued. "When people help create something, they defend it. When it's imposed on them, they find ways around it."

Darius nodded slowly. "So we're not just writing policies. We're building coalitions."

"Exactly. And that approach, making security collaborative rather than dictatorial, is what caught Keystone's attention in the first place."

Maya pulled up the next slide, showing a timeline. "We have a unique opportunity here. Instead of racing to align with their policies, we can invite them into our process. Show them what made us acquisition-worthy to begin with."

She glanced around the room, meeting each person's eyes. "Some of you might end up leading these initiatives. Others might decide this transition is a natural point to explore new opportunities. Either way, what we've built together matters. And how we handle this next chapter will determine whether it survives."

The room fell silent as her words sank in.

"So," Maya said, clicking to the next slide, "who's ready to help me redefine what security collaboration looks like at scale?"

Every hand in the room went up.

* * *

Maya stared out the window of her temporary office as lightning split the sky. The late summer storm matched her mood, turbulent, unpredictable, and brewing with intensity. One month into the merger with Keystone, and everything felt like it was happening at warp speed.

"Do mergers usually go this fast?" she muttered to herself, scrolling through the endless email threads about organizational restructuring. Her calendar had become a battleground of overlapping meetings, integration planning, access reviews, and security harmonization, all while the actual security work still needed to be done.

The question looming over everything: Would she be the CISO for this new combined organization? The thought both thrilled and terrified her.

Doubling her team size, budget, and scope of responsibility would be a career milestone. However, the merged security department was currently a mess of competing priorities and redundant roles.

A knock at her door interrupted her thoughts. James Chen, Keystone's CISO, stood in the doorway with two coffee cups.

"Thought you might need this," he said, offering her one. "Just came from the admin privileges meeting. That was..."

"A complete disaster?" Maya finished for him.

"I was going to say 'spirited,' but your word works too." He took the seat across from her desk. "Too many cooks in the kitchen."

"Too many admins in the system," Maya corrected. "We have people with overlapping privileges across four different identity stores. It's a nightmare waiting to happen."

Thunder boomed outside, making them both glance toward the window.

"The access review redesign is our first real test," James said. "If we mess this up, we'll have black eyes and hurt feelings across the entire technology organization."

Maya nodded, feeling the weight of it. Currently, both security teams are trying to collaborate, but with undefined leadership and unclear decision rights, even simple choices have become committee debates.

"The board isn't making this any easier," she said. "Every decision feels like it's being watched for signs of who's winning, your team or mine."

"When neither of us is winning if we're fighting," James added.

Maya leaned forward. "We need to get back to principles. This merger happened because our approaches complemented each other. Your team's technical depth, our collaborative methodology."

She pulled up a slide deck on her laptop and turned it toward James. "Look at what we did last quarter with our access review process. We included team leads from every department, got their input on pain points, and built a process they actually wanted to follow."

James studied the slides. "This is why we acquired you. Your team's ability to build stakeholder buy-in is exactly what we've been missing."

"Then let's showcase that strength," Maya said, a plan forming. "The access review redesign, let's use it to model how the combined security organization should work."

She stood up and began sketching on her whiteboard. "Instead of our teams fighting over who leads the process, let's demonstrate collaborative leadership. We bring in team leads from across the organization, acknowledge their concerns upfront, and co-create the solution."

James nodded slowly. "Using the integration project itself to demonstrate the value of your approach."

"Exactly. This is where we provide stability and exemplify a smooth transition to the rest of the organization." Maya felt energy replacing her earlier uncertainty. "When people see security leaders collaborating instead of competing, it sets the tone."

"I like it," James said, standing to join her at the whiteboard. "And I think I know who should lead it."

Maya raised an eyebrow.

"You," he said simply. "If we're going to adopt your collaborative approach, you should demonstrate it. I'll support you publicly."

Maya felt a surge of hope. Perhaps this was her answer about the future CISO role, not in words, but in action. By focusing on principles rather than positions, they could build something stronger than either organization had before.

"Let's do it," she said as another flash of lightning illuminated the room. "The storm's not letting up anytime soon, might as well learn to dance in the rain."

* * *

The storm had cleared, leaving behind a week that felt more structured than chaotic. Maya noticed the subtle shift in the hallways, as more people made eye contact, stopped her with questions, and sought her input on integration challenges. The merger was still a tangle of competing priorities, but at least now there was a path forward.

She and James had fallen into an unexpected rhythm. Despite graduating the same year from bitter rival universities, they'd found common ground in their approach to the merger. The irony wasn't lost on Maya, that fall day decades ago, she'd been in the marching band while James had been across the field, a cheerleader with biceps like thighs, both of them hoping to demolish the other. Now they were building something together.

"We should probably never mention the '99 homecoming game," James had joked during their planning session yesterday.

"Probably best for team morale," Maya had agreed with a small smile. Internally, she said in her mind, "Hoot! Growl!"

But today's finance team presentation threatened to disrupt their progress. Maya arrived early to set up her laptop when she noticed something that made her security senses flare. Three finance managers huddled near the whiteboard, passing around a tattered yellow Post-it note.

"Here, use this for the quarterly close system," one whispered. "Don't change it, IT gets pissy when we mess with the passwords."

Maya pretended to focus on her slides while her mind raced. Password sharing was a cardinal security sin, but calling them out now would derail an important meeting and potentially damage the collaborative atmosphere they'd worked hard to create.

She bit her tongue through the presentation, making mental notes as the finance team outlined their merged workflows. The problem was clear: too many systems, too many credentials, and complete uncertainty about which platforms would survive the merger.

"Thanks for your patience as we navigate this transition," the finance director concluded. "We're doing our best to keep operations flowing."

I bet you are, Maya thought, the Post-it note haunting her.

Rather than issuing an immediate mandate, Maya spent the next day engaging in casual conversations with SaaS administrators across both legacy organizations. The pattern was consistent; teams were sharing credentials as a stopgap while the board deliberated on final system selections.

"We know it's not ideal," admitted one admin from Keystone. "But what choice do we have? The board can't seem to put their egos aside long enough to make decisions."

Maya leaned back in her chair, seeing the bigger picture. This wasn't just a security problem; it was an operational necessity born from organizational uncertainty. The finance team wasn't being careless; they were being practical in an impossible situation.

That evening, she sketched out a different approach. Instead of cracking down with password policies that would be ignored, what if she acknowledged the operational constraints and built a solution that addressed both security and business needs?

"Enterprise password management," she explained to James the next morning. "With secure credential sharing capabilities. Teams can share access without Post-it notes, we get proper logging and authentication, and nobody's workflow gets disrupted."

James nodded slowly. "Using their problem to create a better solution."

"Exactly. We also involve the finance team in the design of the implementation. Make them the champions, not the culprits." Maya pulled up a project plan. "If we frame this as solving their pain rather than fixing their mistake, we'll get buy-in across the organization."

"This is why you're becoming the face of security here," James said quietly.

Maya looked up, surprised.

"People trust you because you don't just see violations, you see context. You find solutions that work with how people actually operate."

Maya felt a flutter of pride. By treating the finance team's password sharing not as a compliance failure but as valuable input for a better security architecture, she was demonstrating exactly the collaborative approach the merged organization needed.

* * *

Another week passed, and the password manager implementation showed promising signs. Maya observed the adoption patterns with quiet satisfaction. The finance team's power users had become unexpected evangelists, showing off the mobile app integration during lunch breaks. Meanwhile, a small but vocal contingent of self-proclaimed "analog professionals" grumbled about "yet another system to learn."

"I've been writing my passwords in this notebook for twenty years without any problems," one senior accountant had declared, brandishing a worn leather journal as if it were a holy relic.

Maya's calendar had become a fortress with few openings. The merger's technical integration consumed her days, while policy harmonization filled her evenings. Her apartment had begun to feel like an expensive storage unit, she visited primarily to shower and change clothes.

The digital clock on her dashboard read 10:43 PM as she pulled into her parking spot last night. Maya had sat there for a moment, engine off, staring at the notification stack on her phone. The security alerts never stopped, even when she did.

"You're doing exceptional work," James had told her last week. His words should have been reassuring, but the uncertainty surrounding the executive structure cast a long shadow. The other organization's CISO remained in play, though increasingly absent from key meetings. Maya knew she shouldn't take that as a sign. Corporate chess moved slowly, with pieces often sacrificed when least expected.

At least she wouldn't need to build rapport with a new CFO. Marc Lindstrom had survived the merger shuffle after his counterpart took her golden parachute and a vacation home in Sedona. Small mercies.

Maya arrived fifteen minutes early for the threat modeling session, arranging whiteboards and digital displays with methodical precision. Today's goal: transform threat modeling from a review checkpoint into a design partnership. The stakes felt higher than usual; this approach would set the tone for security integration across both organizations.

"Let's start with the user journey," Maya began once the room filled with product managers, developers, and architects from both legacy companies. "Before we talk about threats, let's understand what we're building and why it matters."

Thirty minutes in, the energy shifted. A product manager from the acquired company crossed his arms.

"With all due respect, we had a perfectly functional security review process before. This feels... excessive." His tone carried the weight of merger fatigue. "We don't have bandwidth for reinventing wheels."

Maya noticed several heads nodding in agreement. The collaborative space she'd hoped to create was contracting, hardening into resistance.

"You're right," Maya said, surprising him. "Your process worked for your organization's size and risk profile. And our process worked for us. But neither will serve us at our new scale."

She stepped away from her position at the front of the room, physically demonstrating her shift from presenter to participant.

"I'm not here to dictate a new process. I'm here because I need your expertise. Our combined attack surface has expanded dramatically, and I don't have visibility into all the business constraints you're navigating."

Maya moved to the whiteboard and wrote: "What would make threat modeling valuable to YOU?"

The room fell silent, then gradually filled with voices, hesitant at first, then gathering momentum.

"If it could help us prioritize tech debt..."

"If we could use it to justify feature trade-offs..."

"If it didn't always happen too late to make meaningful changes..."

As the list grew, Maya noticed the shift. People leaned forward. The energy transformed from defensive to constructive. They weren't being subjected to security; they were helping shape it.

"This is your process too," Maya said, stepping back to survey the collaborative vision taking shape. "Security works best when it's built on collective wisdom, not isolated expertise."

By the session's end, they had sketched a framework that bore little resemblance to either organization's previous approach, something new, something better, something they had built together.

* * *

Maya's phone lit up with a calendar invite as she packed her laptop at the end of the threat modeling session. "Meeting with Elena Park and Martin Wells - CEO Office - 4:30 PM." Her pulse quickened. A Friday afternoon meeting with both CEOs wasn't typical, especially not one scheduled with only two hours' notice.

The rest of the afternoon blurred past. Maya reviewed security metrics, approved two access requests, and barely tasted the protein bar she'd grabbed for lunch. At 4:28, she stood outside Elena's office, smoothing her blazer and taking a centering breath.

Elena's office occupied the northeast corner of the executive floor, with floor-to-ceiling windows offering a panoramic view of the city. Martin Wells, CEO of the acquired company, sat in one of the leather chairs opposite Elena's desk. They both looked up when Maya entered.

"There she is," Elena said, her smile broader than usual. "The woman of the hour."

Maya tilted her head slightly. "I'm not sure what I did to earn that title."

Martin leaned forward. "That threat modeling session today. First time I haven't received complaint emails from my team about merger integration."

"Actually," Elena added, "people from both sides had positive things to say. Technical teams are calling it 'productive' and 'worthwhile', words I haven't heard together since we announced this merger."

Maya settled into the remaining chair, acutely aware of both CEOs studying her. "I'm glad it was valuable for everyone."

"That's what we want to understand," Elena said. "What exactly did you do differently? Because whatever it was, we need more of it."

Maya considered her response carefully. "The key was creating a framework where everyone had legitimate input. Not just token participation, but actual influence over the outcome."

She pulled out her tablet and opened her notes. "I structured it as a workshop rather than a review. Started with business goals instead of security requirements. Used visual mapping to connect security controls directly to product features."

Maya demonstrated how she'd created feedback loops throughout the session, ensuring everyone's concerns were captured and addressed. She explained the importance of shared language and continuous validation.

"Where did you learn this approach?" Martin asked. "It's not standard security methodology."

Maya smiled. "A combination of sources. Some from a mentor who challenges my thinking." She thought briefly of the Gray Hat and his cryptic guidance. "Harvard has excellent free courses on collaborative leadership. Business podcasts during my commute. And honestly, years of learning what doesn't work."

Elena nodded approvingly. "Could you document this process? We need this kind of collaborative framework across all our integration workstreams."

"Absolutely," Maya replied. "The beauty is that it's adaptable to different contexts."

As Maya elaborated on the implementation details, she felt a peculiar sensation, as if she were being watched. She glanced toward the corner of the office and nearly faltered mid-sentence.

The Gray Hat sat there, seemingly invisible to Elena and Martin, one leg crossed casually over the other. He wore his customary black blazer over a faded DEF CON shirt. His expression carried a mixture of satisfaction and calculation, as though watching a chess piece move exactly where he'd anticipated.

Maya maintained her composure, continuing her explanation without betraying her surprise. The Gray Hat's presence unsettled her, but his slight nod of approval sent a contradictory wave of validation through her.

As the meeting concluded, Maya gathered her materials, hyperaware of the Gray Hat's continued observation. His eyes held the look of someone whose plan was unfolding precisely as designed, and somehow, she was central to whatever that plan might be.

* * *

Maya collected her laptop from the conference room table, still absorbing the aftereffects of another successful collaborative session. The product and engineering teams had started the meeting with crossed arms and skeptical expressions. They'd left ninety minutes later with shared ownership of a solution that addressed both security requirements and development constraints.

As she headed toward her office, Maya noticed Jessica Huang lingering by the doorway, clutching her notebook like it contained state secrets. The security intern had been present at both collaborative sessions this week, quietly observing from the corner with an intensity that reminded Maya of herself at that age.

"That was incredible," Jessica said, falling into step beside Maya. "The way you got everyone involved instead of just presenting requirements... they actually wanted to solve the problems by the end."

Maya smiled. "That's the goal. When people help build the solution, they're invested in making it work."

"I noticed you used the same structure as the threat modeling session," Jessica continued, flipping open her notebook. "You started with shared goals, then facilitated instead of directing, and you made sure everyone had input before decisions were made."

Maya slowed her pace, surprised by the intern's astute observations. Jessica wasn't just passively attending these meetings; she was studying them with remarkable precision.

"I've been taking notes on your approach, not just the content," Jessica admitted, a slight flush coloring her cheeks. "The way you build consensus without compromising on security principles, it's not what they taught us about security leadership."

They reached Maya's office, and she gestured for Jessica inside. "What did they teach you?"

"That security is about enforcing standards and ensuring compliance," Jessica replied. "But what you're doing feels different. People aren't just following rules, they're actually invested in security outcomes."

Maya nodded thoughtfully. "Because they helped create them."

Jessica's eyes lit up. "Exactly! When everyone collaborates on solutions, they gain a deeper understanding of the 'why' behind security controls. They're not just following requirements, they're implementing something they helped design."

Maya studied the eager intern, recognizing something familiar in her enthusiasm, a hunger to move beyond textbook approaches to security.

Jessica had seen beyond the technical content to the human dynamics that made security effective.

"I'd love to hear more of your observations during our check-in on Friday," Maya said. "Sometimes fresh eyes see patterns the rest of us miss."

* * *

Jessica beamed at the validation, her shoulders straightening with newfound confidence. "I'll organize my notes before Friday."

Maya leaned against her desk, watching as the intern tucked her notebook away. There was something refreshing about Jessica's earnestness, her ability to recognize the subtle dynamics that many security professionals missed even after years in the field.

"Before you go," Maya said, "there's something else I'd like you to consider over the weekend."

Jessica paused, attention immediately focused. "Of course."

"You've noticed how individual collaborations create effective solutions," Maya began, choosing her words carefully. "That's a critical insight. But there's a larger pattern at work across these sessions that's worth examining."

Maya walked to her whiteboard and drew three overlapping circles. "When we collaborate with the product team, engineering, and legal separately, we create point solutions. But notice what happens when these relationships begin to intersect and reinforce each other."

She shaded the overlapping areas. "These relationship networks, the connections between teams that form around security, create something more powerful than any single collaboration."

Jessica studied the diagram, her brow furrowed in concentration. "A security ecosystem?"

"Exactly. Individual collaborations solve immediate problems, but relationship networks create lasting influence." Maya capped her marker. "When engineering starts advocating for security to product, or when legal references our framework in their vendor reviews without us prompting them, that's when security becomes embedded in the organization's DNA."

Jessica's eyes widened with understanding. "It's not just about solving the problem in front of you, it's about creating connections that solve problems when you're not even in the room."

Maya nodded, impressed. "That's what I'd like you to watch for next week. Not just how we collaborate with each team, but how we're connecting teams to each other through security."

Jessica took out her notebook again, jotting down a few quick notes. "I'll be looking for it. Thank you for the insight, Maya."

As Jessica left, Maya turned back to her whiteboard, adding a few more connecting lines between the circles. The young intern had an intuitive grasp of influence that couldn't be taught in any bootcamp. With the right mentoring, Jessica might someday understand what had taken Maya years to learn: that in security, your greatest asset wasn't your technical knowledge, but your ability to build networks of trust that outlasted any single initiative.

Chapter 8:

Build Coalitions Before You Need Them

Maya stared at her laptop screen, the weekend sun streaming through her apartment window. Her fingers hovered over the keyboard as she organized her thoughts. The news of Keystone's acquisition had thrown everything into flux, but as Jessica's insights reminded her, this wasn't just about surviving change; it was an opportunity to architect it.

She took a sip of tea and opened a new document titled "Coalition Strategy." The traditional approach would be to wait until the acquisition closed, then react to whatever security structure Keystone imposed. But that reactive model was exactly what she'd been fighting against her entire career.

"Crisis-only engagement creates distrust," she typed. "Continuous relationship building creates resilience."

Maya had seen this pattern too many times at FinSecure. Security teams that only appeared during incidents were viewed as the cleanup crew, rather than strategic partners. Those who maintained ongoing relationships became trusted advisors whose input was sought before decisions were made.

She sketched a rough org chart of both TechForward and Keystone, marking key stakeholders and their spheres of influence. James Chen, Keystone's CISO, would be a critical ally, but equally important were the product leaders, finance team, and engineering managers who would shape the integrated company's priorities.

Maya leaned back, considering the fundamental truth she'd learned: security wasn't a technical problem to be solved, but a human system to be influenced. Human systems operate through relationships, not just reporting lines.

She created three columns: "Immediate Coalitions," "Mid-term Allies," and "Long-term Network." Under immediate coalitions, she listed Priya, Luis from Sales, and Rina from Product. Each brought different strengths: Priya's operational excellence, Luis's customer trust perspective, and Rina's product vision. Together, they could demonstrate how security enabled business outcomes rather than blocking them.

"I need to be the connective tissue," Maya murmured, "not just between security and the business, but between business units that don't realize their security interdependencies."

She thought about Malik and Noah's recent collaboration on the Apex client portal. What had started as a security review had evolved into a genuine partnership. Now Malik was getting pulled into design discussions without Maya having to advocate for it.

That was the model, security becoming embedded in workflows not through mandate but through demonstrated value.

Maya added notes about building an integration task force that spanned both companies, positioning security as an enabler of the merger's success rather than a compliance hurdle. She'd need to frame security risks in terms of business impact, not technical vulnerabilities.

"This isn't about defending my territory," she typed. "It's about creating a shared vision of security as business enablement."

As the afternoon light shifted, Maya refined her approach. She would meet with James Chen next week, not to discuss security tools or compliance frameworks, but to gain a deeper understanding of his vision for security's role in Keystone's growth strategy. She'd connect with Marc Lindstrom to frame security investments in terms of revenue protection and acquisition value preservation.

Most importantly, she'd continue building coalitions that would outlast any organizational chart reshuffling. Because in the chaos of integration, influence would flow not through formal authority but through trusted relationships and demonstrated value.

Maya closed her laptop with newfound clarity. She lived in the chaos of cybersecurity every day. Risk was her constant companion. But so was the knowledge that security at its best wasn't about saying no, it was about enabling yes, safely. And that required being a builder of bridges, not just barriers.

Tomorrow, she would begin turning these plans into action. The acquisition wasn't a threat to her security vision; it was the perfect opportunity to demonstrate it.

* * *

Maya gathered her tablet and notes as the leadership team filtered out of the conference room. The past week had been a blur of meetings, each one a carefully calculated move in her coalition-building strategy. She'd connected with developers, product managers, and finance leaders across both companies, positioning security as a business enabler rather than a roadblock.

"Maya, got a minute?" Elena Park's voice cut through her thoughts. The CEO gestured toward her corner office with a smile that didn't quite reach her eyes.

"Of course," Maya replied, following Elena down the hallway.

Elena's office commanded a view of the city skyline, the late afternoon sun casting long shadows across the sleek furniture. Maya noticed the subtle changes, a few Keystone awards now mingled with TechForward's on the credenza, visual evidence of the merger's progress.

"Close the door, would you?" Elena settled behind her desk, fidgeting with a pen. The CEO's usual rapid-fire confidence seemed muted.

Maya sat across from her, sensing the unusual tension. "How can I help?"

"I just got off a call with the board," Elena began, leaning forward. "Your name came up. Multiple times, actually."

Maya kept her expression neutral despite the sudden flutter in her chest.

"They're impressed with how you've been handling the integration planning. Apparently, you've made quite an impression on the Keystone side." Elena tapped her pen against the desk. "Richard specifically mentioned your work with their engineering team on that compliance framework."

"We found a way to meet requirements without slowing their release cycle," Maya explained. "It was just about understanding their constraints."

Elena nodded. "Well, it didn't go unnoticed. The board sees you as a key player in making this merger work." She paused, her gaze shifting to the window. "They've also been discussing the executive structure going forward."

Maya felt her pulse quicken. "I imagine there are a lot of moving pieces."

"There are." Elena's voice dropped slightly. "I wanted to give you a heads-up... I'm hearing that James Chen might be tapped as CISO for the combined organization."

The words hung in the air between them. Maya had considered this possibility in her planning, but hearing it verbalized made it suddenly concrete.

"The board values your approach," Elena continued, studying Maya carefully. "But James has been with Keystone for years, and they're the acquiring company."

"I understand," Maya said, keeping her voice steady. "James is well-respected in the industry."

Elena leaned back in her chair. "I'll be honest, Maya. I'm not entirely sure what this means for your role going forward." A flicker of vulnerability crossed the CEO's face, unusual for the typically confident executive. "The board has confirmed I'll continue as CEO, but they're clearly weighing various leadership configurations."

Maya nodded, processing the complex emotions washing through her. Pride in the recognition her work had received, mixed with uncertainty about her future. The relationships she'd been building weren't just about the present crisis; they were her safety net for whatever came next.

"Thank you for telling me, Elena. I appreciate the transparency."

"You've built something valuable here," Elena admitted. "People trust you. From developers to board members, that's rare." She straightened some papers on her desk. "Whatever happens with titles, that influence doesn't disappear overnight."

Maya recognized the truth in Elena's words. Her strategy hadn't been about securing a position; it had been about creating a network of relationships that transcended organizational charts.

"I'm focused on making this merger successful," Maya said. "The rest will sort itself out."

As she left Elena's office, Maya felt strangely centered despite the uncertainty. She had built bridges throughout both organizations, and bridges, unlike titles, couldn't be simply reassigned.

* * *

Maya's fingers tapped out the message before she could second-guess herself. "Snowcones. 30 minutes." She stared at the screen, watching as the delivery confirmation appeared, followed almost immediately by a thumbs-up emoji. No words needed, their emergency meet-up protocol was well-established.

The riverwalk stretched before her, early evening joggers weaving around tourists. She spotted him immediately, black blazer over a faded conference t-shirt, that weathered Moleskine tucked under his arm. The Gray Hat looked perfectly at ease, as if coincidentally enjoying the evening air rather than responding to her cryptic summons.

"You look rattled," he observed as she approached, no preamble necessary.

Maya leaned against the railing, watching the water ripple below. "I just had the strangest conversation with Elena." She recounted the meeting, the praise from the board, the recognition of her coalition-building, followed by the revelation about James Chen.

"So they value your work, but not enough to keep you as CISO." The Gray Hat didn't phrase it as a question.

"That's what it sounds like." Maya's voice remained steady despite the tightness in her chest. "I've been building relationships across both organizations, proving security can be a business enabler. Just last week, I worked with the finance team to fast-track a critical security investment that would carry over post-merger."

"Impressive."

"And yet." She couldn't keep the edge from her voice. "James Chen gets the job."

The Gray Hat remained silent, his gaze fixed on the horizon.

"What?" Maya finally asked.

"I'm curious if you've asked yourself why this bothers you so much."

Maya felt a flash of irritation. "Because I'm good at what I do. Because I've earned it." She paused. "Because in the back of my mind, I already considered myself the CISO of the combined organization."

"And James?"

"A pretender to the throne," she admitted, then winced at how it sounded.

The Gray Hat nodded, turning a page in his notebook. "Do you want to be the CISO for this new company?"

The question caught her off guard. "Of course I, " She stopped, realizing she wasn't entirely sure. Was that her own doubt, or had he planted it?

"Wait." Maya narrowed her eyes. "You're a consultant for Keystone. What do you know about all this?"

A hint of a smile crossed his face. "I was wondering when you'd ask that."

"And?"

"And I'd be disappointed if you hadn't gotten here eventually." He closed his notebook. "You're a tremendous CISO, Maya. One of the best I've worked with."

"But?"

"Not a 'but.' A 'what's next.' Where do successful CISOs go after they've proven themselves?"

The question lodged in her mind. Had she asked it, or had he? It didn't matter; she couldn't shake it now.

"The board sees something in you that transcends the CISO role," he continued. "They've noticed how you build coalitions, translate security into business value, and navigate complex organizational dynamics."

Maya stared at the water below, watching the current's patterns shift and change. "You're saying there's something bigger."

"I'm saying great security leaders often outgrow security leadership." He shrugged. "Just something to consider."

They walked in silence for several minutes before parting ways. As Maya headed home, she realized she had fewer answers than when she'd arrived, more questions spinning through her mind, and yet, strangely, a sense that things might unfold in ways she hadn't imagined.

The uncertainty that had felt threatening now felt like a possibility. Whatever happened with titles, she had built something no one could take away, influence that extended beyond organizational charts, relationships that transcended roles.

Maybe losing the CISO position wasn't an end. Maybe it was an opening.

* * *

Steam curled from Maya's teacup as she gazed out at her garden sanctuary. Morning light filtered through the courtyard, catching on the dew-kissed leaves of her potted herbs and the climbing jasmine she'd coaxed up the lattice. The patio wasn't large by suburban standards, but in the city, this private green space was her refuge, her thinking spot.

She sank deeper into her wicker chair, letting the week's tension unravel. The conversation with the Gray Hat still echoed, but from this distance, it felt less like a crisis and more like a crossroads.

Maya's thoughts drifted to her early career days, before gh05t5c1pt, before CISO, when she was just another anxious analyst trying to make security matter. The Meridian project had nearly broken her. Week after week of security recommendations ignored, vulnerability reports filed away, her carefully crafted policies gathering digital dust.

"I'm done," she had told her mentor over lunch. "I'm going back to coding. At least developers build things people actually want."

Her mentor had simply raised an eyebrow. "Who says security can't build things people want?"

That conversation changed everything. The next day, instead of writing another ignored security bulletin, Maya approached the sales team. They were losing deals because they couldn't answer security questionnaires fast enough.

"What if we built something together?" she had proposed. "Automation that pulls from our security documentation, pre-populates answers, and flags what needs human review?"

Their eyes had lit up. Suddenly, security wasn't the department of "no"; it was a partner in winning business.

Maya sipped her tea, remembering the late nights coding that tool, the sales director bringing her coffee, the collective celebration when they closed their first enterprise deal with the new system. Security went from blocker to enabler. Her title hadn't changed, but her influence had.

That project became "our challenge" instead of "her requirement." The coalition she built became her first real taste of organizational influence, providing security through collaboration rather than control.

Maya set down her cup, watching a hummingbird dart between her flowering plants. Perhaps losing the CISO title wasn't as big a setback as it seemed. The real power had never been in her title, but in the coalitions she'd built, the trust she'd earned, the value she'd created across boundaries.

The hummingbird paused, suspended in midair, before zipping away to new territory.

* * *

Monday morning found Maya sitting in TechForward's cafeteria, scanning the room with fresh eyes. What had once been just faces and job titles now represented potential connections in a larger web of influence. The merger with Keystone was moving forward, and while her CISO role hung in limbo, Maya saw opportunity where others might see uncertainty.

She spotted Luis from Sales hunched over his laptop, furiously typing. His team was preparing for their first joint pitch with Keystone's sales force. Maya grabbed two coffees and made her way over.

"Looks like you could use this," she said, sliding a cup toward him.

Luis glanced up, surprised. "Maya. Thanks. This security questionnaire from the hospital network is driving me crazy. Fifty-three questions about our data retention policies alone."

"Mind if I take a look?" Maya pulled up a chair without waiting for an answer. "I've been thinking, what if we created a shared repository between our teams and Keystone's? Their compliance documentation is stellar, and we could leverage their certifications while we get ours up to speed."

Luis's expression shifted from one of stress to one of intrigue. "You think James would go for that?"

"I already floated the idea with him yesterday. He's interested in whether we can make it work operationally." This wasn't entirely true; she hadn't spoken to Keystone's CISO yet, but she knew she could sell it.

"That would be... incredible. When can we start?"

"I'll set up a working session this week. And Luis? Bring your toughest objections from clients. I want to build this around what you actually need."

By Wednesday, Maya had created three additional strategic touchpoints. She spent an hour with Rina from Product, discussing how to harmonize the security review processes between the merging companies. Instead of dwelling on which approach would win, Maya focused on designing something better than either company could have done alone.

"The beauty is that we can start fresh," she told Rina over lunch. "No legacy baggage. Just smart defaults that make security seamless."

Rina nodded slowly. "You're not fighting for territory like everyone else."

"I'm fighting for something better," Maya replied. "A security function that enables velocity instead of hindering it."

That afternoon, Maya invited Rebecca from HR to coffee. While others focused on organizational charts, Maya saw Rebecca as the keeper of company culture, a critical ally in building security awareness.

"People are anxious about the merger," Rebecca confided. "They're worried about job security, new processes, different expectations."

Maya leaned forward. "What if we turned security into a unifying force? Not just systems security, but psychological safety. Clear guidelines,

109

transparent processes, shared understanding of how we protect each other and our customers."

Rebecca's eyes lit up. "That's... not what I expected from the security team."

"Maybe that's the problem," Maya said with a smile. "We've been too predictable."

By Friday, Maya had mapped out an informal coalition spanning both companies, product managers, engineers, HR specialists, and sales executives. She didn't have a title for what she was building, but she knew it transcended traditional security boundaries.

In her one-on-one with Priya, Maya shared her emerging vision.

"You're building a shadow security organization," Priya observed, both impressed and concerned.

"I'm building bridges," Maya corrected. "If James becomes the CISO, he'll need these relationships to succeed. If it's me, I'll need them too. Either way, the company wins."

"And if it's neither of you?"

Maya smiled. "Then we've still created something valuable, a network that understands security isn't a department, it's a shared responsibility. That's bigger than any org chart."

As she walked back to her desk, Maya felt a curious lightness. For the first time in her career, she wasn't defining herself by a title or position. She was becoming something more fluid, more influential, a connector of people and possibilities, a translator between worlds.

Whatever came next, she was building the coalition before she needed it.

* * *

Maya was midway through her third merger integration meeting of the day when Elena appeared in the doorway, gesturing with a subtle head tilt. The CEO's expression was unreadable, but there was something different in her posture, less tension, more curiosity.

"Maya, got a minute?" Elena asked when the meeting wrapped.

They walked in silence to Elena's office, where the board member from their previous encounter sat comfortably, examining something on his tablet. He looked up and smiled.

"Maya, this is officially Richard Kwan. You two met briefly last week." Elena closed the door behind them. "Rich sits on three other tech boards and has shepherded more mergers than anyone I know."

Richard extended his hand. "Please, call me Rich. I've been hearing interesting things about your... approach."

Maya shook his hand, noting the careful way he'd chosen his words. "My approach?"

"Your coalition," Elena clarified, dropping into her chair. "Several board members have noticed that despite all the chaos of this merger, certain teams are functioning with unusual cohesion. When we traced the common thread, it led back to you."

Rich leaned forward. "I've overseen seventeen acquisitions in my career. I recognize the standard patterns, territorial battles, information hoarding, and paralyzed decision-making. But what's happening in pockets of this organization is different."

"I'm just trying to keep security functioning during the transition," Maya said carefully.

Elena laughed. "Cut the modest act, Park. You've created an influential network that transcends departmental boundaries. The board is curious how you're doing it."

Rich nodded. "More specifically, I'd like to understand your methodology. This isn't accidental."

Maya glanced at the whiteboard covering one wall of Elena's office. "May I?"

"Please," Elena waved her toward it. "You're a whiteboard person. So am I. My son says it's common among neurodiverse people, but I don't know what he's talking about. He's the autistic one, not me."

Maya uncapped a marker, feeling a familiar calm settle over her. Whiteboards were her medium, a canvas where complex ideas became visible, tangible.

"I start with stakeholder mapping," she explained, drawing concentric circles. "But not the traditional kind where you just identify decision-makers." She labeled the inner circle 'Core Collaborators,' the middle 'Connectors,' and the outer 'Context Providers.'

"Core Collaborators are the people directly involved in security decisions. Connectors are those who don't own security but whose work intersects with it significantly. Context Providers are those who hold valuable institutional knowledge or represent important perspectives."

Rich watched intently as Maya added names to each circle, drawing lines between them.

"The key is understanding what each person values," Maya continued, switching to a green marker. "Not just their professional objectives, but what makes their work meaningful to them."

She wrote beside Luis's name: Wants to close deals without compromising integrity.

Beside Rina: Needs to ship features while maintaining customer trust.

"This isn't about manipulation," Maya emphasized. "It's about authentic alignment. I don't approach these relationships thinking 'what can they do for security?' I ask 'How can security help them achieve what matters to them?'"

Elena nodded slowly. "You're creating reciprocity without quid pro quo."

"Exactly. Then I map opportunities for value exchange." Maya drew a matrix on another section of the board. "These are moments where security can provide something meaningful, maybe it's data that helps the sales team respond to customer concerns, or expertise that helps engineering avoid a costly rework."

Rich stood up and approached the whiteboard. "This is fascinating. You're essentially creating security ambassadors without formal authority."

"I prefer to think of it as distributing security ownership," Maya replied. "The formal security team can't be everywhere. But if people throughout the organization understand how security connects to their goals, they become extensions of our function."

Elena studied the diagram. "And all of this without a formal mandate."

"Sometimes influence works better without one," Maya said quietly.

Rich exchanged a glance with Elena. "I think we need to talk more about this approach, Maya. It has implications far beyond the security function.".

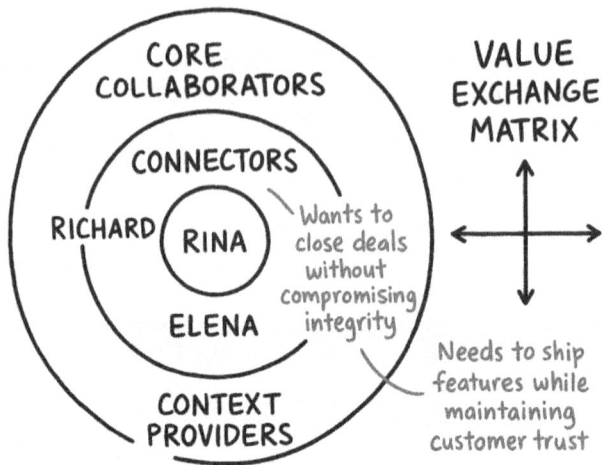

CORE COLLABORATORS

CONNECTORS

RICHARD RINA

ELENA

CONTEXT PROVIDERS

VALUE EXCHANGE MATRIX

Wants to close deals without compromising integrity

Needs to ship features while maintaining customer trust

* * *

Maya stepped out of Elena's office, her mind still processing the unexpected interest from the CEO and board member. The whiteboard diagram had revealed more of her approach than she'd initially planned, but their genuine curiosity had drawn it out of her. She took a deep breath, centering herself before heading back to the security operations center.

"So, that looked intense," Priya said, materializing beside her with suspicious timing. She matched Maya's pace down the hallway, her casual tone belied by the alertness in her eyes.

"Were you waiting for me?" Maya asked, a slight smile playing at her lips.

"Me? No, just happened to be... reviewing camera feeds. For security purposes." Priya's poker face cracked into a grin. "Fine. The team's been buzzing since you got called to the principal's office. What did Park want?"

Maya glanced around before responding. "Apparently, our coalition-building has caught the board's attention."

"Our what now?" Priya's eyebrows shot up.

"The relationships we've been cultivating across departments. The way information flows to us before problems escalate." Maya pressed the elevator button. "They noticed the pattern."

Priya nodded slowly. "You know, you remind me of General Karim from my Army days."

"Should I be flattered or concerned?" Maya asked as they stepped into the empty elevator.

"Definitely flattered. He was this quiet force who somehow got everyone to run toward the hardest problems, and they'd do it willingly." Priya leaned against the elevator wall. "He never shouted orders. He just... connected people to purpose."

The elevator doors opened, and they continued toward the SOC.

"That's the secret most security leaders miss," Maya said. "Relationships aren't just about being liked. They're intelligence networks that warn you about threats before they materialize. They're support systems when you need emergency resources."

"And they're shields when politics get ugly," Priya added. "Which brings me to what's really on everyone's mind."

Maya tilted her head questioningly.

"The CISO position," Priya said bluntly. "Team's worried. If it's not you, many people aren't sure they want to stick around. James is great, but..."

"But he's not building what we're building," Maya finished the thought.

They paused outside the security operations center. Through the glass, Maya could see the team working, analyzing alerts, and collaborating on investigations; the rhythm of a well-functioning security unit she'd helped shape.

"James knows what he's doing," Maya said carefully. "And whatever happens with the CISO role, what we've built goes beyond any single position."

"That's some Zen master stuff, but people want to know if you're fighting for it," Priya pressed.

Maya turned to face her directly. "I'm fighting for something more important, a security function that has influence regardless of who holds which title." She lowered her voice. "The relationships we've built? The trust we've earned? That doesn't disappear with an org chart change."

"You really believe that?"

"I do," Maya said firmly. "The most powerful security teams aren't the ones with the biggest budgets or the fanciest titles. They're the ones that have woven themselves into the fabric of the organization, the ones that people turn to because they want to, not because they have to."

Priya studied her face for a moment. "Okay. I'm in. But fair warning, the team might need to hear this directly from you."

Maya nodded, pushing open the door to the SOC. "Then let's talk to them. Because our strength isn't in our hierarchy, it's in our network."

* * *

Maya scanned the security operations center, noting the mix of focused concentration and furtive glances in her direction. Word traveled fast in security teams; they were trained to notice patterns, after all.

"Can I get everyone's attention for a few minutes?" she called, her voice carrying just enough to be heard without sounding like an announcement.

Heads turned, keyboards fell silent. The team gathered around, some perched on desks, others leaning against walls. Their faces held a mixture of curiosity and concern.

"I know there's been talk about leadership changes," Maya began, meeting their eyes one by one. "And I wanted to take a moment to reflect on something more important than titles."

She moved to the whiteboard and drew a simple network diagram, nodes and connections forming a web.

"This is us," she said, tapping the center node. "And these are all the relationships we've built across the organization." She labeled the connections: Finance, DevOps, Legal, Marketing, Product, IT. "These aren't just lines on a board. They're pathways of influence we've created together."

Maya turned back to face the team. "When Amir got that 3 AM call from DevOps about the deployment pipeline issue, they didn't call because it was in some runbook. They called because Amir had spent time understanding their challenges and had proven he could help without judgment."

Amir nodded, a slight smile crossing his face.

"When Priya spotted that unusual pattern in customer authentication, she didn't just escalate it through formal channels. She reached out directly to Serena in Fraud because they'd built trust during that cross-functional project."

"The fraud team still brings us cookies every month for that catch," Priya added.

Maya continued, "What we've built goes beyond procedures and policies. We've created a network that gives us visibility, influence, and impact regardless of our position on an org chart." She paused. "And that's something no reorganization can take away."

She erased the diagram and drew a simple triangle. "Security sits at an interesting intersection. We see across the organization in ways others don't. That visibility gives us power, but only if we use it wisely."

"Political awareness isn't about playing games," Maya said, her voice softening. "It's about understanding how decisions really get made, knowing who influences whom, and recognizing when formal authority differs from actual influence."

She looked around at her team, pride evident in her expression. "You've all internalized these principles. I've watched you build relationships before you needed them. I've seen you translate technical concepts into language that resonates with different teams. You've led with empathy instead of alerts."

Maya took a breath before continuing. "I also want to be clear about something. James is an excellent CISO. He has vision, technical depth, and leadership skills that have served this organization well."

Several team members exchanged glances, but Maya continued steadily.

"This team is in good hands with James. And more importantly, this team is in good hands because of all of you, because you understand that security influence comes from how we work, not just what we know."

She smiled, seeing recognition in their faces. "Whatever happens with organizational changes, remember this: the principles we've practiced together have made you more than security professionals. They've made you trusted advisors. And that influence remains, regardless of who has which title."

The tension in the room had visibly dissipated. Shoulders relaxed, postures straightened.

"Now," Maya concluded, "let's get back to protecting this place, not just with our tools and technologies, but with the relationships and trust we've built together."

Chapter 9:

Navigate Politics with Awareness, Not Avoidance

Maya watched the executives file into the boardroom, each taking their customary places around the mahogany table. After weeks of observing these integration meetings, she'd developed an informal map of the alliances and tensions that truly governed decisions, regardless of what the merger org chart suggested.

"Security people hate politics," The Gray Hat had once told her. "They think it's beneath them, corrupting their technical purity."

"Isn't it?" she'd asked.

"Politics is just the operating system of human organizations," he'd replied. "You wouldn't deploy code without understanding the environment it runs in, would you?"

The memory brought a faint smile to her face as she took her seat across from James. His presence at these meetings, occupying the same CISO role she did, created an awkwardness neither of them acknowledged openly. The board hadn't made their final decision yet, leaving both of them in a professional limbo that tested Maya's composure daily.

She opened her notebook, thinking about her early days as a security architect. The cloud migration initiative she'd championed had been technically flawless, with airtight controls, comprehensive monitoring, and perfect compliance alignment. And it had failed spectacularly.

Not because of any technical flaw, but because she hadn't recognized that the VP of Engineering had staked his reputation on the on-premises infrastructure. She hadn't seen how the CFO's bonus structure disincentivized the capital expenditure shift. She hadn't understood that the CIO needed a win after the previous quarter's outages.

The technical merits hadn't mattered because she'd misread the human environment completely.

"We'll begin with the security integration update," said Eleanor, the board chairwoman. "James, would you start us off?"

Maya noted the subtle positioning in that choice, and who speaks first always mattered in these settings. She watched James deliver a polished presentation on the threat landscape and mitigation strategies. His approach was direct, authoritative, focusing on worst-case scenarios and technical solutions. The room's energy shifted as he spoke, some leaning forward with concern, others back with skepticism.

When her turn came, Maya deliberately chose a different angle.

"Building on what James outlined, I'd like to connect these security considerations to our three core business priorities," she began, noticing how the CEO's attention immediately sharpened. "Our market expansion in APAC faces specific regulatory hurdles that security can actually accelerate, not just protect."

She moved through her points methodically, watching the room's dynamics. The COO, who had been checking his phone during James's presentation, was now taking notes. The new board member from the acquiring company, whom Maya had earlier identified as the quiet kingmaker, was nodding slightly.

Maya hadn't compromised her security principles. She'd simply translated them into the language and priorities that mattered to this specific audience. This wasn't manipulation; it was communication with context.

As the meeting progressed, the faction lines became increasingly visible. Two board members consistently reinforced James's points while another group subtly amplified Maya's perspective. The CEO remained deliberately neutral, though Maya caught the slight approving nod when she connected security controls to customer trust metrics.

This wasn't the petty politics she'd once disdained. This was organizational awareness, understanding the currents that would either carry her initiatives forward or sweep them away.

When Eleanor called for final comments, Maya chose her words carefully.

"Security works best when it's aligned with how the organization actually functions, not just how we wish it would function," she said. "Our integration plan acknowledges both the technical requirements and the operational realities of our teams."

As the meeting adjourned, Maya gathered her materials, conscious of the shifting alliances around her. The Gray Hat had been right. Understanding politics wasn't selling out; it was simply recognizing that security decisions, like all decisions, happened in a human context.

And in that context, relationships and perception mattered just as much as technical merit.

* * *

Maya spotted James lingering in the conference room after the others had filed out. She took a deep breath, recognizing the opportunity. The tension between them had been building since the merger announcement, with each meeting serving as a subtle competition for the single CISO position that would remain.

"James, got a minute?" Maya closed the door behind her. "I think we should talk."

He looked up, wariness evident in his posture. "About the integration report?"

"About us. This situation." Maya gestured between them. "Look, I've been thinking about what's happening here. We're both talented security leaders, but right now we're playing a zero-sum game that security itself is losing."

James's expression shifted from guarded to curious. "I'm listening."

"The board sees us as competitors, but what if we approached this differently?" Maya pulled out a chair across from him. "What matters most isn't which one of us ends up with the title. What matters is that security becomes the foundation this merged company builds on."

James nodded slowly. "That's... refreshingly direct."

"You noticed something in that meeting I've been tracking, too," Maya continued. "The formal power structure, the org chart, isn't where the real decisions are happening. Richard and Eleanor have the titles, but it's actually the COO and that quiet board member from Keystone who are steering things."

"I picked up on that, too," James admitted. "The COO barely acknowledged my technical points but was writing furiously during your business alignment section."

"That's exactly it," Maya leaned forward. "Security decisions here aren't made based on who has the most comprehensive threat model. They're made based on who understands the unofficial priorities and unspoken concerns."

James's posture relaxed slightly. "At Keystone, I always focused on the technical excellence. I figured the rest would follow."

"I used to believe that, too," Maya smiled. "But I learned the hard way that being right technically doesn't automatically make you effective organizationally."

"So what are you suggesting?" James asked.

"A joint approach. We combine your technical depth with my stakeholder navigation. We present a unified security strategy that addresses both the formal requirements and the informal concerns." Maya drew a quick diagram showing their complementary strengths. "We stop competing and start collaborating."

James studied the diagram, then looked up with newfound respect. "This could actually work. If we map the real influence networks together..."

"Exactly. We identify who really drives decisions, what they actually care about, and how security can enable those priorities, not just protect them."

As they sketched out their joint strategy, Maya realized this wasn't just about securing their professional futures; it was also about securing their personal futures. It was about applying the very principles she'd been learning: coalition-building, political awareness, and focusing on outcomes rather than ego.

By the time they finished, they had more than a plan. They had a partnership.

* * *

Maya glanced at the spreadsheet on her monitor, then back at James across her desk. The autumn sunlight filtered through the blinds, casting grid-like shadows across their budget projections. Three months of partnership had transformed their relationship from cautious competitors to a formidable team.

"We need to understand the rhythm of this place," Maya said, tapping her pen against the desk. "TechForward's budget cycle was predictable. Keystone's is... not so much."

James nodded. "Richard tends to make funding decisions based on quarterly performance rather than annual planning. It's more reactive."

"That's exactly the kind of insight we need." Maya stood and walked to the whiteboard where they'd mapped out the organizational structure. "The formal process says budget requests go through Marc in Finance, but..."

"But Eleanor from the board has been vetoing technology investments that don't show immediate ROI," James finished.

Maya circled Eleanor's name. "Right. And she's particularly focused on the integration costs from the merger."

They'd spent weeks identifying the hidden power dynamics of the newly merged organization. The org chart showed one reality, but their careful observation revealed another. Maya had cultivated relationships with administrative assistants, while James had leveraged his technical credibility with the engineering leads. Together, they'd assembled a more accurate map of how decisions really flowed.

"What if we frame our security investments around merger risk mitigation?" Maya suggested. "Not as costs, but as protections for the integration itself."

James's eyes lit up. "That speaks directly to Eleanor's priority. We could show how security enables faster, safer system integration."

"And we should get Anika from Legal involved early," Maya added. "She carries weight with the board on compliance matters."

They continued refining their approach, identifying which executive would respond to which framing. Technical risk for the CTO. Revenue protection for Sales. Operational continuity for the COO.

"This isn't just about getting budget," Maya realized aloud. "It's about translating security into the language of each stakeholder's priorities."

James smiled. "Security as a business enabler, not just a cost center."

Maya nodded, feeling a quiet pride in how far they'd come. What had started as political awareness had evolved into something more powerful: the ability to align security with the organization's most vital concerns. Not by avoiding the politics, but by navigating them with purpose.

"Let's get to work," she said. "We have allies to recruit and a budget to secure."

* * *

Three weeks later, Maya watched James pace the length of her office, his confidence from their budget victory now replaced with visible frustration. Their security vendor selection process had hit a political minefield that no spreadsheet could resolve.

"Eleanor wants to go with SecureStack because of their cost structure," James said, running a hand through his hair. "But the CTO is pushing for TechGuard because their API integrates better with our existing systems."

Maya leaned back in her chair. "And let me guess, Sales is lobbying for VaultSec because their biggest client uses it?"

"Exactly." James dropped into the chair opposite her desk. "I thought our political mapping would make this easier, but it's just exposed how many competing interests we're dealing with."

Maya nodded, studying James's face. He'd come so far from the technically brilliant but politically naive CISO she'd first met. Now he was seeing the full complexity of organizational dynamics, sometimes more clearly than she'd like.

"Welcome to the next level," she said. "It's not just about understanding the politics. It's about balancing interests that are fundamentally in tension."

James slumped. "So what do we do? Pick the most powerful stakeholder and hope the others fall in line?"

"That's one approach," Maya acknowledged, "but it burns political capital you might need later." She stood and walked to her whiteboard, where their stakeholder map had grown increasingly complex. "There's another way."

She circled three names. "Instead of choosing sides, we need to reframe the conversation. What if we shift from 'which vendor' to 'what outcomes do we need from any vendor?'"

Understanding dawned on James's face. "Create a unified set of requirements that satisfies everyone's core needs."

"Exactly." Maya handed him a marker. "Let's identify what each stakeholder truly cares about, beyond their vendor preference."

They worked through each executive's underlying concerns. Eleanor worried about unexpected costs. The CTO needed technical compatibility. Sales wanted customer confidence.

"Now comes the hard part," Maya said. "We need to have individual conversations with each stakeholder. Not to convince them, but to understand their non-negotiables."

Over the next two days, James met with each key player. Maya observed from a distance, impressed by how he'd learned to listen for what wasn't being said. He no longer led with solutions but with questions that revealed deeper priorities.

In the final selection meeting, Maya watched James work the room with a newfound political fluency.

"I've spoken with each of you about your priorities," he began. "And I believe we've found a path forward that addresses everyone's core needs."

He presented a hybrid approach: TechGuard's platform with a negotiated pricing structure similar to SecureStack's, plus a partnership with VaultSec for customer-facing documentation and compatibility.

"This isn't about compromise," James continued. "It's about optimization. Eleanor gets predictable costs. Engineering gets its technical integration. Sales gets the customer confidence they need."

Maya noticed the subtle nods around the table. James had given each stakeholder ownership of a piece of the solution while creating something better than any single vendor could provide.

After unanimous approval, James caught Maya's eye across the conference room. No words were needed. He had navigated competing interests not by avoiding politics, but by transforming them into collaborative problem-solving.

Later, as they walked back to their offices, Maya smiled. "You know what you did in there?"

"Applied what you taught me about political awareness?"

"More than that," Maya said. "You showed them that security isn't just about technology, it's about finding solutions that work for the entire business."

James nodded. "I'm starting to think the best security leaders are actually translators."

"And diplomats," Maya added. "Never forget the diplomacy."

* * *

Maya was still basking in the afterglow of James's successful vendor negotiation when she noticed Richard Kwan hovering near the conference room exit. The board member's typically composed demeanor seemed off, his jaw clenched, shoulders rigid.

"Maya, a word?" His tone carried an edge she'd never heard before.

"Of course." She followed him to a small meeting room, mentally cycling through possible concerns. Budget? Timeline? The new compliance framework?

Richard shut the door with more force than necessary. "I'm getting tired of this."

"I'm sorry?" Maya's mind raced, searching for context.

"This whole coalition-building approach you've implemented." He gestured vaguely. "It's undermining the proper channels of authority."

Maya blinked, genuinely confused. Richard had always been supportive of her work. "I'm not sure I understand. The vendor selection process just went through proper channels, and everyone seems pleased with."

"That's exactly it." He cut her off. "Everyone's pleased except those of us who built this company's governance structure. The board used to have direct oversight of major security decisions. Now we're just rubber stamps for these... consensus agreements you orchestrate."

The realization hit Maya like a cold wave. While she'd been mapping stakeholders across departments, she'd overlooked the power dynamics on the board itself. Richard wasn't just any board member; he'd been the security committee chair before Keystone's acquisition.

"Richard," she said carefully, "I had no idea you felt sidelined."

"Of course not. You've been too busy making everyone else feel included." His voice carried years of accumulated frustration. "I have three decades of experience in this industry. I wrote the security governance playbook for Meridian prior to joining here. But apparently my input isn't valuable in this new collaborative utopia."

Maya took a deep breath, resisting the urge to defend herself. This wasn't about being right; it was about understanding what Richard really needed.

"You're absolutely right that I've missed something critical," she said, meeting his gaze directly. "Your experience is exactly what we need, especially as we integrate these new systems."

The admission seemed to catch him off guard. His posture softened slightly.

"What specifically concerns you about our current approach?" she asked.

Richard paused, as if weighing whether to continue his frustration or engage. "The vendor selection framework lacks the risk oversight perspective that only comes with board-level experience. These collaborative decisions prioritize operational convenience over governance."

Maya nodded. "That's a significant gap I hadn't considered." She pulled out her notebook. "Would you be willing to help me address it?"

The simple act of taking notes visibly shifted something in Richard's demeanor.

"What if we created a governance advisory function?" Maya suggested. "Not to slow decisions, but to ensure we're considering long-term risks that might not be visible at the operational level."

Richard leaned forward slightly. "That could work, if it's substantive and not ceremonial."

"It would need your leadership," Maya said. "No one else has your perspective on governance models that balance oversight with operational needs."

By the time they left the meeting room thirty minutes later, they had outlined a governance framework that would provide Richard with meaningful input while preserving the collaborative approach that was working well with the operational teams.

As they parted ways, Richard stopped. "I appreciate you listening, Maya. Most people just try to convince me I'm wrong."

Maya smiled. "Sometimes the people who seem like blockers are actually just experts waiting to be included."

Walking back to her office, Maya made a note to update her stakeholder map. She'd been so focused on building bridges across departments that she'd missed the shifting power dynamics above her. The lesson was clear: political awareness wasn't just about understanding today's influence networks, it was about recognizing when yesterday's power structures still cast shadows.

* * *

Two days after the encounter with Richard, Maya found Priya waiting in her office. The SOC director leaned against the window, her usual practical dark attire contrasting with the afternoon sunlight streaming in behind her.

"So," Priya said without preamble, "I heard you turned Richard Kwan from adversary to advocate in under an hour." She folded her arms. "That's impressive, even for you."

Maya smiled. "News travels fast."

"That's my point." Priya sat down across from Maya's desk. "I've been watching you navigate all these political minefields for months now. The vendor selection, the budget fight with Marc, even getting Tariq to actually listen to security concerns." She tapped her fingers on the armrest. "I want to know how you do it."

Maya raised an eyebrow. "You've never been interested in the political side before."

"I never thought I needed to be." Priya's expression turned thoughtful. "I always figured good technical work would speak for itself. But after seeing how you've transformed our influence here... I'm starting to think differently."

"About?"

"About my career path." Priya met Maya's gaze directly. "I'm considering the CISO track now. But I need to understand how you map all these competing interests and priorities so effectively."

Maya nodded, recognizing the significance of this moment. Priya had always been technically brilliant but politically avoidant.

"First thing I do is create an actual stakeholder map," Maya said, pulling out a notebook. She sketched a quick diagram. "Not just formal reporting lines, but informal influence channels too. Who talks to whom? Who trusts whom? Who has historical alliances?"

Priya leaned forward. "Like an adversary map, but for the organization."

"Exactly. I update it quarterly, or whenever there's a major shift." Maya tapped the diagram. "Then I overlay competing priorities. Product wants speed, Finance wants predictability, Legal wants defensibility."

"And how do you balance those when they conflict?"

"I don't try to eliminate the conflict, that's impossible. Instead, I look for the shared interest beneath the surface positions." Maya drew connecting lines between different stakeholders. "Richard wasn't actually against collaboration. He was against losing his voice in governance. Once I understood that, we could find a solution that preserved both."

Priya nodded slowly. "In the military, General Karim used to say, 'Know the terrain before the battle.' I guess this is the corporate equivalent."

"There's more to it," Maya continued. "You need to understand decision cycles. Budget requests fail not because they're bad ideas, but because they arrive at the wrong time. Every organization has rhythms, quarterly reviews, annual planning, and product releases."

"So you time your proposals to align with those cycles?"

"And I frame them in the language of whatever's most important in that cycle. During growth periods, I talk about enablement. During cost-cutting, I focus on risk efficiency."

Priya wrote notes in her precise handwriting. "This is like learning a whole new discipline."

"It is. But remember, this isn't manipulation, it's translation. The core truth about security risks doesn't change, but how you present it does." Maya smiled. "The good news is you already have the hardest skill to teach."

"Which is?"

"Integrity. People trust you because you're straight with them. Political awareness without integrity is just manipulation. With integrity, it becomes effective leadership."

Priya looked at her notes, then back at Maya. "I always thought becoming a CISO meant becoming less technical. But it's actually about becoming more strategic about how you apply that technical knowledge."

Maya nodded. "Exactly. The technical expertise is your foundation. The influence skills are how you ensure that expertise actually matters."

* * *

Priya's brow furrowed. She tapped her pen against the notebook. "But this all feels... I don't know, manipulative? Like social engineering but aimed at our colleagues instead of adversaries."

Maya leaned back in her chair, considering her response carefully. This wasn't the first time she'd heard this concern.

"I understand that hesitation," she said. "But think about it this way, persuasion and influence on their own aren't unethical. They're tools, like any other in our arsenal."

"Tools can be misused," Priya countered.

"Absolutely. The same hammer that builds a house can end a life." Maya leaned forward, resting her elbows on her desk. "The tool itself is neither ethically good nor bad. What the person holding it does with it determines the ethicality."

Priya seemed to absorb this, her sharp eyes focused on some middle distance as she processed.

"When I map stakeholders and their interests, I'm not looking for ways to trick them. I'm looking for legitimate common ground where their goals and security can coexist." Maya gestured to the diagram between them. "That's why integrity matters so much. Without it, this becomes manipulation. With it, it's strategic alignment."

"So where's the line?" Priya asked. "Between ethical influence and manipulation?"

"Intent and transparency," Maya answered without hesitation. "I never hide my security objectives. I'm clear about what we need and why. But I take the time to understand what others need too, and find the intersection."

Priya nodded slowly. "Like when you convinced the dev team to implement MFA. You didn't hide that it was for security, but you framed it around protecting their code integrity."

"Exactly. That wasn't manipulation, it was translation into something they already valued." Maya smiled. "The best influence happens when people make good decisions for their own reasons, not just because security said so."

"That's what I've always struggled with," Priya admitted. "I want people to do the right thing because it's the right thing."

"They will," Maya said. "But 'right' looks different depending on where you sit. A product manager's 'right thing' includes shipping on time. Our job isn't to override their priorities, but to show how security enables them."

Priya's expression shifted from skepticism to thoughtful consideration. "So ethical influence is about alignment, not control."

"Precisely. And that's the difference that matters."

* * *

Maya watched Priya's expression shift from skepticism to understanding. She recognized that moment, the exact instant when a conceptual framework clicked into place. It was the perfect time to plant a seed.

"You know that isn't all you need to be an effective CISO, right?" Maya asked, gathering her notes from the table.

Priya looked up, her brow furrowing slightly. "What do you mean?"

"Political awareness helps you navigate the organization," Maya said, leaning against her desk. "But that's only half the equation. Operational excellence makes your work worth supporting in the first place."

"Like what we did with the SOC redesign?" Priya asked.

Maya nodded. "Exactly. You can have all the influence in the world, but if your operations are chaotic, if your team can't deliver consistently, that influence evaporates." She tapped her finger on the stakeholder map they'd created. "This gets you a seat at the table. What you bring to that table determines whether they'll invite you back."

Priya seemed to absorb this, her eyes drifting to the whiteboard where they'd mapped out the quarter's initiatives.

"When I was at FinSecure," Maya continued, "I watched a brilliant CISO lose everything because he couldn't manage workflow. Great vision, terrible execution. The business lost faith."

"I've always been strong on the operational side," Priya said.

"You have," Maya agreed. "But there's a difference between running operations and optimizing them for influence. It's about making security work visible, predictable, and aligned to what the business values most."

Maya didn't know what her future looked like at TechForward, not with the Keystone acquisition looming, but she knew Priya had CISO potential. Whatever time she had left, she wanted to make sure Priya was ready.

"Monday," Maya said, gathering her bag, "let's talk about how to manage workflow, not just work volume. I think you're ready for that conversation."

Priya nodded, a small smile playing at the corner of her mouth. "I'll bring coffee."

As they walked out together into the Friday evening, Maya felt a quiet satisfaction. The seeds were planted. Whether she remained at TechForward or not, something valuable would grow.

Chapter 10:

Manage Workflow,

Not Just Work Volume

Maya's phone lit up with a Signal notification. It was Ricky Lim, a name she hadn't seen pop up in weeks.

"Can we talk?" The message was followed by a string of emojis: a fire, an ambulance, and a person with their head exploding.

Maya smiled. Classic Ricky drama. She typed back: "Call in 5?"

Her phone rang almost immediately.

"Maya, I'm drowning." Ricky's voice had the hollow quality of someone who hadn't slept properly in days. "Three months into this CISO gig, and it's a disaster. Everyone warned me this place burned through security leaders, but I thought I could fix it."

Maya moved to her balcony, watching the evening traffic below. "What's happening?"

"Everything. Compliance backlog, three audits running simultaneously, understaffed SOC, shadow IT everywhere." His words tumbled out. "The team is amazing, smart, dedicated, but we're just... stuck. We patch one hole, three more appear. I haven't made it home for dinner in two weeks."

Maya recognized the pattern immediately. It was the same trap she'd fallen into during her first year at TechForward, and what the Gray Hat had helped her escape.

"You're drowning in volume, not flow," she said quietly.

"What?"

"You're trying to do everything at once. That's why nothing's getting done." She leaned against the railing. "Remember when General Karim used to say, 'Amateurs talk tactics, professionals talk logistics'? Security is the same way. Amateurs focus on threats. Professionals focus on workflow."

"Flow," Ricky repeated. "That's what I'm missing. It feels like we're just reacting to everything."

Maya thought about her upcoming session with Priya. "There are four types of work in security: planned business projects, internal improvement, change management, and unplanned work. Most teams drown because unplanned work consumes everything else."

"That's us," Ricky sighed. "One emergency after another."

"Here's what the Gray Hat taught me: don't just track what work you're doing, track how work moves through your system." Maya closed her eyes, visualizing the framework. "What's your WIP limit?"

"My what?"

"Work in progress limit. How many initiatives can your team actually handle simultaneously?"

The silence told her everything.

"That's your first step," Maya continued. "Figure out your capacity, limit your work in progress, and make the backlog a negotiation tool, not a guilt trip. When someone wants to add something, ask what comes off."

Ricky's breathing had slowed. "That... actually makes sense. We're trying to do thirty things at 10% instead of three things at 100%."

"Exactly. Start visualizing your workflow. Make it visible to everyone. Then focus on reducing the handoffs and wait states." Maya smiled. "I'm teaching Priya this on Monday. Why don't you join us? We'll do a working session."

"Really? You'd do that?"

"Of course. You helped me when I was stuck at FinSecure." Maya remembered how Ricky had covered for her during that massive incident response. "Besides, I need someone to help demonstrate to Priya that this isn't just theory."

"I'll be there," Ricky said, his voice steadier now. "Even if I have to fake a doctor's appointment."

After they hung up, Maya opened her notebook to the page where she'd started planning Monday's session with Priya. She added Ricky's name and a new section: "Case Study: Transforming Reactive Security into Strategic Flow."

She thought about how differently Priya and Ricky approached problems, Priya with methodical precision, Ricky with creative energy. Having them both in the room would create a perfect dynamic tension. They'd push each other to think differently.

Maya smiled as she sketched out the agenda. The Gray Hat had always said the best way to internalize a lesson was to teach it to someone else. Monday's session wouldn't just help Ricky and Priya; it'd crystallize everything she'd been learning about operational excellence.

The best influence didn't come from telling people what to do. It came from helping them discover solutions on their own.

* * *

Maya had initially planned a small workshop for Monday with just Priya and Ricky. But word traveled fast at TechForward. By Thursday, her calendar invite had ballooned from three participants to twenty-seven.

"What happened?" Maya asked Rebecca from HR, who'd stopped by her office.

Rebecca smiled. "I may have mentioned it to Elena during our one-on-one. She thought it sounded interesting and forwarded it to the leadership team."

Maya's phone buzzed with a new email. She glanced down and nearly dropped it.

"Richard Kwan from Keystone's board just RSVP'd," she said, her voice rising slightly. "And he's bringing James Chen, their CISO."

"Is that a problem?" Rebecca asked.

Maya took a deep breath. "No. Just... unexpected. This was supposed to be a working session, not a presentation."

But by Monday morning, Maya had transformed the small conference room booking into the main auditorium. She arrived early to arrange the tables in small groups rather than classroom-style rows. On each table, she placed markers, sticky notes, and a laminated card with the four types of work.

Priya arrived first, eyebrows raised at the setup. "I thought we were just helping Ricky?"

"Change of plans," Maya said. "Apparently, workflow management is the hot new thing."

People began filtering in, first her security team, then product managers, developers, and finally, the executives. Maya spotted Richard Kwan and James Chen slipping into seats at the back. Elena Park gave Maya an encouraging nod from the front row.

"Welcome ,everyone," Maya began once the room had settled. "I'm honestly surprised to see so many of you here today. This was originally going to be a small working session on managing security operations, but clearly there's broader interest."

She clicked to her first slide: MANAGE WORKFLOW, NOT JUST WORK VOLUME.

"Every team in this room is drowning in work. But the problem isn't volume, it's flow. When everything is a priority, nothing gets done well. Today, we're going to learn a framework that's transformed how my team operates."

Maya gestured to the cards on each table. "There are four types of work in any organization. Business projects, the things that drive revenue and growth. Internal improvements, the investments in your own capabilities. Change management, the planned maintenance and updates. And finally, unplanned work, the fires, the incidents, the emergencies."

She clicked to a pie chart showing a typical distribution.

"Most teams spend 80% of their time on unplanned work, leaving scraps for everything else. But unplanned work is a symptom, not just a reality. It often comes from postponing the other three types."

From the back, Richard Kwan leaned forward. Maya caught his eye and continued.

"I'd like each table to map your current work. What percentage falls into each category? Where are your bottlenecks? What happens when new priorities emerge?"

The room hummed with conversation. Maya circulated, listening to discussions at different tables. Tariq and Noah were having an animated debate about whether technical debt counted as unplanned work or internal improvement. Marc from Finance was explaining to Anika from Legal how budget cycles created artificial spikes in business projects.

At Priya and Ricky's table, Maya paused longer. Priya had methodically created a detailed flow diagram of the SOC's work processes, while Ricky was rapidly filling sticky notes with all his team's current commitments.

"This is eye-opening," Ricky said. "We're not just overloaded, we're structurally misaligned. Look at all these handoffs between teams."

After twenty minutes, Maya called the room back together. "What did you discover?"

Elena raised her hand first. "My calendar is 90% unplanned work. I'm constantly in reactive mode, which means strategic initiatives keep slipping."

"We found we're starting too many things and finishing too few," added Rina from Product. "Our work in progress is out of control."

From the back, James Chen spoke up. "At Keystone, we implemented WIP limits across all security functions. It was painful at first, saying no is hard, but our completion rate tripled in six months."

Richard nodded beside him. "The board started getting predictable updates instead of constant surprises. That built tremendous trust."

Maya smiled, sensing a perfect teaching moment. "That's exactly it. Workflow isn't just about efficiency; it's about trust. When you can predict your capacity and deliver consistently, you build credibility."

She clicked to her final slide: a simple kanban board with clearly marked WIP limits.

"This isn't just a security principle. It's an organizational one. Limit your work in progress. Make your work visible. Manage the flow, not just the volume. This creates the space for both strategic work and continuous improvement."

As the workshop wrapped up, Maya noticed Richard Kwan making his way toward her. This impromptu session had unexpectedly become one of the most important presentations of her career, all because she'd been willing to share a simple framework that transcended security.

Sometimes influence came from the most unexpected places.

* * *

Maya stared out at the park's pond, the amber and crimson leaves reflecting in the water. Steam rose from her coffee cup, warming her hands against the autumn chill. Beside her, the Gray Hat sat quietly, his own mug cradled between weathered palms.

"I still can't believe what happened back there," Maya said finally. "Richard Kwan and James Chen taking notes at my impromptu workshop? Elena actually implementing something I suggested?"

The Gray Hat smiled but said nothing, watching a duck glide across the water's surface.

"The funny thing is," Maya continued, filling his silence, "I've been using that framework with my team for months. Categorizing work types, limiting WIP, and visualizing flow. But I never thought to share it beyond security."

"Why not?" The Gray Hat's question was simple but piercing.

Maya considered this. "I guess I thought it was just... how I managed my team. Not something worth teaching others."

"And yet," he observed, "when you did share it, everyone from the CEO to the board members leaned in."

The realization hit her. "I've been hoarding knowledge, haven't I? Keeping my methods to myself when they could have been helping others all along."

The Gray Hat nodded slightly. "You transformed your security team by making their work visible and manageable. Today, you gave others the tools to do the same."

Maya watched the ducks, thinking about how her team had changed after implementing flow management. Predictability had replaced chaos. Trust had replaced skepticism. They'd gone from firefighters to strategists.

"I liked it," she admitted. "Seeing the light bulbs go on across departments. Watching Ricky realize why his team was drowning."

"It's a different kind of influence," the Gray Hat said. "Not securing systems, but securing understanding."

"Is that what you do?" Maya asked suddenly. "All those cryptic comments about Tokyo last month and São Paulo next week?"

The Gray Hat smiled. "Sometimes. I help people see what they already know but haven't recognized. Different contexts, different challenges, but the principles remain the same."

Maya took a sip of coffee, considering this path she hadn't imagined. Teaching others to see differently. Building capability, not dependency.

"I never thought about consulting," she said. "But there's something powerful about helping others find their own solutions."

"The best teachers," the Gray Hat replied, "don't give answers. They create the conditions for discovery."

The ducks paddled lazily as Maya sat with this thought, watching the autumn leaves drift onto the pond's surface.

* * *

Maya looked up from her monitor as a knock sounded on her office door frame. Priya stood there with a pink box in one hand and a coffee in the other, wearing an expression Maya rarely saw, something approaching excitement.

"Brought the team donuts," Priya said, flipping open the box lid. "Figured you deserved first pick after yesterday's workshop."

Maya selected a chocolate glazed. "Thanks. Everything okay in the SOC?"

"Better than okay." Priya set the box down and leaned against the doorframe. "I've been thinking about what you did yesterday. That workflow framework you showed everyone."

"What about it?" Maya took a bite, watching Priya carefully.

"I've been working for you for almost a year, and I never realized..." Priya shook her head. "You've been running our team this way the whole time, haven't you? The work categorization, the WIP limits, the visualizations, it's all been happening right under my nose."

Maya brushed sugar from her fingers. "I didn't make a big deal about it. Just implemented it quietly."

"That's your way, isn't it?" Priya smiled slightly. "But here's the thing, I think we could take it further in the SOC. Our alert triage process is still too reactive. We're always drowning in volume."

Maya nodded. "What are you thinking?"

"Different work cadences for different types of work." Priya's eyes lit up. "Critical alerts get immediate response, but what if we batch the low-severity ones? What if we schedule regular blocks for proactive hunting instead of squeezing it in whenever alerts slow down?"

"Go on." Maya leaned forward.

"And the pen tests and audits, we always scramble when they hit. But they're predictable events. We could build capacity planning around them." Priya paced the small office. "The threat intel team is always complaining they can't get detection engineering time. What if we created a flow where threat intel feeds directly into detection-as-code pipelines?"

Maya smiled. "Sounds like you're thinking about applying Lean principles to create Agile workflows."

"Exactly!" Priya stopped pacing. "Detection-as-code could follow the same workflow as our developers. Write it, test it, deploy it, monitor it. Continuous integration for security detections."

"The developers would love that. Speaking their language."

Priya nodded vigorously. "And it would give us predictability. Right now, the team is just responding to whatever's loudest. There's no rhythm, no cadence."

Maya took another bite of her donut, considering. "You know what impresses me most about this?"

"What?"

"You're not just thinking about making your life easier. You're thinking about how to make the entire security function more effective."

Priya looked down for a moment. "I've spent years focusing on tools and technical skills. But watching you yesterday... I realized maybe the most powerful tool is how we organize our work."

"It's a different kind of leverage," Maya agreed. "Not just working harder, but working smarter."

"I want to try implementing this with my team," Priya said. "Maybe start with a kanban board for alert triage, then expand to other work types."

Maya nodded. "Start small, show results, then scale. Classic change management."

"Would you..." Priya hesitated. "Would you help me think through the implementation? Not run it, just advise."

Maya felt a warmth that had nothing to do with the sugar and caffeine. This was the Priya she'd been hoping to see: strategic, forward-thinking, ready to lead change rather than just manage crises.

"I'd be happy to," Maya said. "But I think you already know what to do."

* * *

Maya stood at the whiteboard in the conference room, surrounded by security leadership from both TechForward and Keystone. The merger announcement had been made three weeks ago, and this was their second integration planning session. Sticky notes covered the board in a rainbow of colors, each representing a different security function, tool, or backlog from both companies.

"We've identified forty-three overlapping tools between our organizations," Maya said, gesturing to the blue cluster. "Everything from duplicate SIEMs to three different vulnerability scanners."

James Chen, Keystone's CISO, nodded. "And seventeen redundant roles across our combined teams."

The room fell silent. Everyone knew what redundancies typically meant during mergers.

Maya stepped back from the board. "I want us to think differently about this situation. This isn't just about cutting costs or picking winners and losers. This is our opportunity to reimagine how security operates."

She walked to the red section of sticky notes, the combined backlog of security issues. "Look at this. Between our two companies, we have over three hundred open security items. Some dating back eighteen months."

Priya leaned forward. "Most executives see backlogs as failures, things we haven't fixed yet."

"Exactly," Maya said. "But what if we reframed them as negotiation tools instead?"

James raised an eyebrow. "What do you mean?"

"Our backlogs tell a story about where we've been investing and where we haven't," Maya explained. "They're evidence of the trade-offs that have been made, often without security's input."

She began rearranging the sticky notes, grouping them by business impact rather than technical severity. "Instead of talking about CVEs and CVSS scores, what if we presented these issues in terms of business risk portfolios?"

Priya caught on immediately. "Like investment portfolios. Some risks you accept, some you mitigate, some you transfer."

"And some you leverage," Maya added. "For instance, these twenty-seven items all relate to our customer data pipeline. That's not just a technical vulnerability, it's a trust issue that affects customer retention."

James stood up and joined Maya at the board. "So instead of begging for resources to 'fix security problems,' we're inviting executives to make informed risk decisions about business assets."

"Exactly," Maya said. "And when we frame it that way, the conversation changes from 'Why haven't you fixed this yet?' to 'How should we invest our limited resources?'"

One of the Keystone managers spoke up. "But how do we actually implement this approach? Most executives' eyes glaze over when we talk about security backlogs."

"We translate," Priya said firmly. "No technical jargon. We talk about time-to-market impacts, revenue protection, and competitive advantage."

Maya nodded. "And we bring options, not problems. For every risk portfolio, we present multiple approaches with different resource requirements and business outcomes."

James studied the board thoughtfully. "This merger gives us leverage we wouldn't normally have. Leadership expects changes during integration. They're primed for new approaches."

"And they're looking for synergies," Maya added. "If we show how consolidating our tools and aligning our teams can both cut costs and improve security posture, that's a win-win they can't ignore."

Priya pulled out her tablet and began taking notes. "We should map each backlog item to a specific business objective. Show how addressing, or not addressing, each item affects those objectives."

"And we need to show the opportunity costs," James added. "If we invest here, we can't invest there. Make them partners in the prioritization."

Maya smiled, watching the energy in the room transform. What had started as an anxiety-filled discussion about redundancies had become a strategic planning session. The backlog wasn't a burden anymore; it was a business tool.

"Let's draft this proposal for the executive team," Maya said. "But remember, we're not asking for approval to fix security issues. We're offering them a framework for making better risk decisions."

James nodded. "From gatekeepers to guides."

"Exactly," Maya said. "We're not the department of no. We're the department of 'how.'"

* * *

Maya sat in the polished boardroom, watching with quiet amazement as Richard Kwan, the Keystone board member who had once questioned her entire approach to security, presented the implementation plan for the merged security organization.

"By categorizing work into four distinct streams, operational, project-based, compliance, and innovation, we create predictable capacity," Richard explained, gesturing to a slide that looked remarkably similar to the model Maya had proposed months ago. "Each stream has its own WIP limits and dedicated time allocation."

Maya caught Priya's eye across the table. Her colleague raised an eyebrow slightly, the ghost of a smile playing at her lips. They both recognized their own ideas being presented back to them, only now with Richard's enthusiastic endorsement.

"The key insight here," Richard continued, "is that we stop pretending security teams can do everything at once. When we limit work in progress, we actually increase throughput and quality."

Elena Park, TechForward's CEO, nodded approvingly. "And the business impact?"

"Measurable improvement in three areas," Richard replied. "First, predictable delivery timelines for security services. Second, faster incident response. And third, increased capacity for strategic work because we're not drowning in operational chaos."

Maya watched the faces around the table. The merger is expected to be finalized next week. Redundancies were inevitable. Her position was one of the most obvious duplications, as James Chen was already serving as Keystone's CISO.

"I'm particularly impressed with this visualization dashboard," Marc Lindstrom, the CFO, commented. "Showing workflow rather than just backlog volume changes the entire conversation."

Maya had built that dashboard. It had taken three iterations and countless late nights with her team. Now it was being presented as part of the new company's strategic direction, without any mention of its origin.

"There's one more component we should discuss," James said unexpectedly. All eyes turned to him. "This entire approach was pioneered by Maya and her team. The transformation in how security operated at TechForward is what caught our attention in the first place."

The room fell silent. Maya felt a flush of surprise.

"In fact," James continued, "I'd like to propose that Maya lead the implementation of this model across the merged organization. We need her expertise to make this work."

Richard nodded slowly. "I agree. This requires someone who understands both the theory and practical application."

Maya sat straighter, mind racing. This wasn't just professional courtesy; it was an opportunity. Not to keep her title, but to expand her impact.

"I'd be honored," she said simply. "But only if Priya co-leads the operational integration. Her hands-on experience is irreplaceable."

As nods of agreement circled the table, Maya realized something profound: her influence had transcended her position. Her ideas were moving forward, with or without her title, because they worked. And that was the most powerful validation of all.

* * *

Back in Maya's office, Maya sank into her chair, still processing the boardroom exchange. The windows framed the afternoon skyline, casting a golden light that caught the edges of the buildings, as if highlighting the possibilities ahead.

"What just happened in there?" Maya asked, looking at Priya, who was leaning against the doorframe.

Priya closed the door and dropped into the chair opposite Maya's desk. "Honestly? I'm not sure. One minute we're preparing for redundancy, the next minute they're asking you to lead implementation."

"Am I still the CISO?" Maya wondered aloud, tapping her pen against the notepad where she'd been sketching the new organizational structure.

"Are you asking me? Because I don't know if I'm still SOC lead either." Priya's laugh carried a note of genuine uncertainty. "But whatever just happened, I think we need to capitalize on it before anyone changes their mind."

Maya nodded, already reaching for her phone. "Let's book time with the Gray Hat. And Elena. We need to understand what this means operationally."

"Add Richard to that list," Priya suggested. "He seemed genuinely impressed with the flow management approach. I've never seen a board member that excited about security operations before."

Maya paused, a realization dawning. "You know what's interesting? When we presented this as a 'security thing,' we got polite nods. But when Richard framed it as a business optimization strategy..."

"Everyone perked up," Priya finished. "Even Marc from Finance was taking notes."

"What if we could do this across the business?" Maya's voice quickened with excitement. "The same principles, categorizing work, setting WIP limits, visualizing flow, they apply everywhere."

Priya leaned forward. "That's exactly what the Gray Hat meant about effectiveness versus effort. We've been focused on doing security work better, but maybe our real value is in how we approach work itself."

"The merger might be the perfect opportunity," Maya said. "Everyone's expecting disruption anyway. We could introduce these flow concepts as part of the integration strategy."

"And suddenly we're not just security people," Priya said, "we're operational effectiveness consultants who happen to specialize in security."

Maya smiled, seeing the path forward with surprising clarity. "I don't care what my title is. This is about impact. And I think we just found our way to make security matter in ways we never imagined."

* * *

Maya glanced around the park bench area. Fall had painted the trees in brilliant reds and golds, and a light breeze scattered leaves across the pathway. She watched Priya's confused expression with amusement.

"So, you just hang out here at the park?" Priya asked the Gray Hat, who sat cross-legged on the bench wearing his customary black blazer over a faded conference t-shirt. "What about when it gets colder?"

"The cold keeps conversations efficient," he replied with a slight smile. "And it's harder for people to eavesdrop when they're shivering."

Maya pulled out her tablet, displaying their latest workflow metrics. "The tiger team approach is working better than I expected. Dev teams are actually asking us to help them optimize their security review processes now."

"Because we're not just telling them what to fix," Priya added. "We're showing them how to work smarter. The WIP limits were genius, teams are finishing security tasks faster because they're not context-switching between fifteen different priorities."

The Gray Hat nodded, watching a squirrel dart across the path. "And what happens next?"

"We scale it," Maya said confidently. "We've proven the model works with three teams. Now we expand to the rest of the organization."

"I was thinking we could create a playbook," Priya suggested. "Standard templates for different work types, visual workflow boards, "

"What do you think it will be like," the Gray Hat interrupted quietly, "when you make secure behavior the path of least resistance?"

Maya froze, her fingers hovering over her tablet. "Wait, what?"

Priya's brow furrowed. "We're optimizing workflows, not behavior."

"Are you sure?" The Gray Hat leaned forward. "When people follow your new processes, what happens to the security decisions they make?"

Maya felt a sudden shift in her perspective, like a camera lens snapping into focus. "They... make better ones. Because we've removed the friction."

"Exactly," he said. "You're not just making security work flow better. You're making secure behavior easier than insecure behavior."

Priya's eyes widened. "So we're not just process engineers."

"No," Maya whispered, the implications unfurling before her. "We're behavior designers."

Chapter 11

Make Secure Behavior the Path of Least Resistance

The Keystone boardroom gleamed with polished mahogany and fresh optimism. Maya scanned the faces around the table, James Chen nodding approvingly at the latest metrics, Elena Park studying the quarterly projections with sharp focus, and Marc Lindstrom actually smiling at security's contribution to client retention. Three months after the merger, things felt surprisingly... stable.

"And that's our implementation progress across all business units," Maya concluded, sliding her tablet toward Priya. "The tiger team approach has exceeded expectations."

Priya took over seamlessly. "We've reduced security review times by 67% while increasing throughput by 41%. More importantly, teams are requesting our involvement earlier in their development cycles."

James leaned forward. "The developer feedback is remarkable. I've never seen engineering teams this positive about security initiatives."

Maya and Priya exchanged a quick glance. Their transition from CISO and SOC lead to leading this specialized tiger team had raised eyebrows initially, but the results spoke for themselves. They weren't managing people anymore; they were managing workflows, and it was working.

"What's the secret ingredient?" Elena asked, tapping her pen against the table. "We've tried security initiatives before, but they always fizzled after the initial push."

Priya shifted in her seat, then let out a small laugh. "I've been thinking about this, and I'm just going to let my intrusive thoughts out; convenience drives behavior more than compliance."

The room went quiet.

"Go on," James encouraged.

"We keep talking about implementing tools, but that's not what's working," Priya continued. "What's working is that we've made secure behavior easier than insecure behavior. People aren't choosing security because we convinced them, they're choosing it because we removed the friction."

Maya felt a surge of excitement. "Exactly. The adoption of password managers jumped from 23% to 91% when we integrated them directly into the workflow. Not because we had better training, but because we made it the path of least resistance."

"The secure code pipeline is getting used because it's faster than the old way," Priya added. "The developers aren't thinking 'I should be secure', they're thinking 'this is just how we work now.'"

Elena nodded slowly. "So you're saying we should focus less on making people care about security and more on making security the convenient choice?"

"People will always take the path of least resistance," Maya said. "So our job isn't to fight human nature, it's to design systems where the easiest path is also the most secure one."

* * *

Elena's office carried the sparse, intentional aesthetic of someone who moved too quickly to collect clutter. She perched on the edge of her desk as Maya and Priya settled into the chairs opposite her.

"I want to dig deeper into this friction concept," Elena said. "If it's working this well, I need to understand it better."

The door swung open and Richard Kwan strode in, his tall frame filling the doorway. "Hope you don't mind if I join. That boardroom discussion caught my attention."

Maya exchanged a quick glance with Priya. Richard's presence meant this conversation had just escalated from tactical to strategic.

"Of course," Elena gestured to the remaining chair. "Maya was about to explain why convenience trumps security awareness."

Maya took a breath, organizing her thoughts. "It's about cognitive load. Everyone has a finite amount of mental energy each day. Security decisions compete with everything else people need to think about."

"Like productivity targets," Elena added.

"Exactly. When security requires extra steps or slows people down, it creates friction. And humans instinctively avoid friction." Maya leaned forward. "Think about your own behavior. Do you ever ignore update prompts because you're in the middle of something important?"

Elena laughed. "Only about fifty times a week."

"That's not because you don't care about security," Maya continued. "It's because in that moment, the friction of interrupting your workflow outweighs the perceived benefit of the update."

Richard crossed his arms. "So awareness training is useless?"

"Not useless," Priya interjected. "But insufficient. Knowledge doesn't automatically change behavior when the environment works against it."

Maya nodded. "We've been designing our systems backward. We build technical controls, then add friction-heavy security requirements, then try to motivate people to push through that friction with awareness programs."

"Instead of designing systems where secure behavior is the default path," Richard mused.

"Exactly. Our secure code pipeline succeeded because we made it faster than the alternative. The password manager took off when we embedded it directly in the workflow." Maya gestured with her hands as she spoke. "We didn't have to convince anyone, we just made security the path of least resistance."

Elena tapped her pen thoughtfully. "So what's the practical application? Beyond the examples you've already implemented?"

"We're working on a new approach to access management," Priya said. "Instead of making people request permissions and wait for approval, we're creating context-aware access that automatically grants appropriate permissions based on role and project."

"Sounds risky," Richard raised an eyebrow.

"Less risky than what happens now," Maya countered. "When access is too restrictive, people find workarounds, sharing credentials, creating shadow IT. By making the secure path more convenient, we actually reduce risk."

Elena stood and walked to her whiteboard. "I see three principles here: identify friction points, redesign for convenience, measure behavior change rather than awareness." She wrote each point as she spoke.

"And involve users in the design process," Maya added. "They know where the friction is better than we do."

Richard leaned back in his chair. "This isn't just about security tools, is it? It's about how we design every business process."

Maya felt a surge of excitement. "Exactly. Security isn't a separate layer we add on top; it's how we design the entire user experience."

"This could transform our product approach, too," Elena said, eyes brightening with possibility. "Making security invisible to users while strengthening our competitive advantage."

"That's the goal," Maya said. "When security becomes the path of least resistance, it stops being the enemy of productivity and becomes its enabler instead."

Richard nodded slowly. "I think we've been solving the wrong problem all along."

* * *

Maya watched Tariq and Rina exchange puzzled glances. The confusion on their faces was evident as the product meeting veered off its intended course for the third time.

"You're not the boss of me," Tariq said with a half-smile that didn't quite reach his eyes. "This was supposed to be about the Apex client portal timeline."

Maya raised her hands in a placating gesture. "You're absolutely right. I didn't mean to hijack the agenda." She glanced at Rina, the Director of Product. "Rina, please continue with your update."

But Elena leaned forward, her eyes bright with interest. "Before we move on past this path of least resistance concept. I keep thinking about how we could apply it to the Apex portal's authentication flow."

Richard nodded enthusiastically. "And Luis mentioned that three prospects specifically asked about security features during demos last week. That never used to happen."

Rina tapped her pen against her notebook. "Our competitors are starting to advertise their security posture. Meridian's latest campaign is all about 'trust by design.'"

Maya felt a curious mix of pride and discomfort. The tiger team's work integrating security into business workflows had created unexpected momentum, but she hadn't intended to derail Rina's meeting.

"What if we repositioned Apex as our first security-embedded product?" Luis suggested, appearing in the doorway. "Marketing's already drafting messaging around it."

"I didn't invite you to this meeting," Rina said, but there was no heat in her words.

Priya caught Maya's eye and raised an eyebrow slightly. This wasn't the first time their security initiatives had spread beyond their control. The context-aware permissions model was now being championed by the HR department. The secure code pipeline had become Dev's favorite new toy.

"Look," Maya said, "this is clearly resonating, but I don't want to disrupt your product roadmap. What if we schedule a separate session to explore security as a product differentiator?"

"Too late," Elena said with a laugh. "The idea's already out there. It's like a virus, the good kind."

Maya recognized what was happening. She'd seen it before when ideas found fertile ground. Security wasn't being forced upon these teams anymore; they were claiming ownership. The friction-reduction approach had become their idea now, not security's mandate.

"Rina," Maya said, "you should lead this conversation. Your product expertise is what matters most here."

Rina looked thoughtful for a moment, then nodded. "Actually, I think there's something to this. What if we formed a small working group to explore security as a competitive advantage?"

The idea had taken on a life of its own. Maya couldn't help but smile. The path of least resistance had become the path most desired.

* * *

Maya looked up from her laptop as Priya appeared in her doorway, coffee in hand and an expression of bewilderment on her face. Priya closed the door behind her and dropped into the chair across from Maya's desk.

"What is going on now?" Priya asked, setting her mug down. "I just sat through the entire platform architecture review, where Tariq spent twenty minutes talking about 'security as a competitive advantage.' I didn't even have to open my mouth."

Maya leaned back in her chair, a small smile playing at the corners of her lips. "I think this is what success feels like."

"It's unsettling," Priya said, but there was warmth in her voice. "You know what Xander told me yesterday? The SOC got three incident reports from Marketing. Marketing, Maya. They've never reported anything before."

"The new simplified reporting system?"

Priya nodded. "That's just it. The new SOC lead shared something fascinating with me. Since we eliminated the twenty-question form and replaced it with just three questions and removed blame language, reporting has increased by 340%. People are flagging things they would have ignored before."

Maya felt a wave of satisfaction. "Remember when we couldn't get anyone to report suspicious emails?"

"Now they're sending screenshots in Slack before we even know about the campaign." Priya took a sip of her coffee. "One of the customer success reps found a vulnerability in the client portal yesterday, and instead of ignoring it, she documented it, reported it, and suggested a fix. She's not even technical."

"Removing friction from security is creating something I never thought I'd see," Maya said, shaking her head slightly. "People actually want to participate."

"It's almost like they care," Priya said with mock astonishment. "When I was in the Army, General Karim used to say that when you make doing the right thing easy and rewarding, people will surprise you with their initiative."

Maya nodded. "We spent years trying to force behavior change through policy and training. All we had to do was make security the path of least resistance."

"And now we have an army of security champions we didn't even have to recruit," Priya said. "I don't know whether to be thrilled or worried that we're working ourselves out of a job."

Maya laughed. "Don't worry. We'll always have plenty to do. We've just moved from pushing the boulder uphill to steering it in the right direction."

* * *

Maya settled into her chair at the polished mahogany table, still not quite believing what she was witnessing. Richard Kwan, Keystone's most intimidating board member, was walking the executive team through a slide deck titled "Security as Competitive Advantage: The Frictionless Experience."

"The numbers speak for themselves," Richard said, gesturing to a graph showing incident reporting trends. "By removing unnecessary friction from security processes, we've created a culture where everyone participates in our security posture. This isn't just good practice, it's becoming a key differentiator in client conversations."

Maya caught Priya's eye across the table. Just six months ago, they'd been fighting for budget scraps. Their approach was now being showcased as a strategic advantage. The boulder wasn't just rolling; it had momentum all its own.

Elena Park nodded appreciatively. "Our sales team tells me the security questionnaire response rate has improved by 40% since implementing these changes. Clients are noticing."

"And worth noting," Marc Lindstrom added, tapping his pen against his notepad, "the cost of incident response is down 28% quarter-over-quarter. When people report early, we catch things before they become expensive."

Maya's attention drifted to a figure sitting quietly in the corner of the boardroom. The Gray Hat was there, observing with that enigmatic half-smile she'd come to recognize. He wore a blazer over a bright pink DEF CON shirt that somehow looked perfectly appropriate despite the formal setting. No one else seemed to notice him, or if they did, they didn't question his presence.

He caught her eye and gave her an almost imperceptible nod. Maya felt a surge of pride. This wasn't just about security metrics anymore; this was about transforming how the entire organization approached risk and trust.

"We're adding this to the annual report," Richard continued. "Our competitors are still talking about their SOC 2 compliance. We're talking about how security enables velocity and builds customer confidence."

Tariq leaned forward. "The engineering teams have stopped viewing security as a checkpoint and started seeing it as a competitive feature. That's a cultural shift I never thought I'd see."

Maya smiled to herself. The Gray Hat had been right all along. When you make security the path of least resistance, you don't just reduce risk, you transform the conversation entirely.

* * *

Maya pulled her jacket tighter against the early morning chill, watching her breath form small clouds in the air. The pond stretched before them, its surface rippling with the gentle breeze. Beside her, Priya huddled deeper into her coat, clearly uncomfortable with their outdoor meeting spot.

"You know," Priya muttered, "when I finally run my own mentoring sessions, they'll be in a wine bar. In the basement of a used bookstore. With heating."

Maya laughed. "The Gray Hat insists this is how it's done. Something about clarity of thought in nature."

The man in question sat cross-legged on a bench nearby, seemingly impervious to the cold. His eyes followed a pair of mallards gliding across the water, steam rising from his coffee cup. He hadn't spoken a word since they'd arrived fifteen minutes ago.

"The most important takeaway," Maya continued, picking up their earlier thread, "is that design shapes behavior more effectively than any training ever could. When we stopped fighting human nature and started working with it, everything changed."

Priya nodded. "People will always choose the path of least resistance. We just had to make that path the secure one." She stamped her feet against the cold. "So what comes next? The tiger team approach worked, but guerrilla warfare isn't sustainable long-term."

Maya had been asking herself the same question. TechForward had transformed from a security disaster into a case study for effective risk management. The board was happy, the teams were collaborating, and for the first time in years, security wasn't seen as the department of no.

"I've been thinking about that," Maya said carefully. "About what's next for both of us."

The Gray Hat glanced over, his eyes crinkling with interest before returning to the ducks.

"I got a call from Ricky Lim last week," Maya continued. "Remember him from FinSecure? He took over as CISO at Meridian six months ago."

"The competitor that's been struggling?" Priya asked.

"The same. They're growing fast, but their security foundation is shaky. Ricky asked if I knew anyone who could come in as a director and help turn things around." Maya paused. "I thought of you."

Priya's eyes widened. "Me? But I've never, "

"You're ready," Maya said firmly. "You understand the technical side better than anyone, but more importantly, you've learned how to translate that into business impact. The team respects you. And after what we've accomplished here, you have a playbook."

The Gray Hat sipped his coffee, watching a new group of ducks land on the pond with a splash. His silence somehow felt encouraging.

"I don't know," Priya said, but Maya could see the wheels turning. "What about you? What comes next for the great Maya Tran?"

Maya smiled. "I'm staying. There is still work to be done here, and the Keystone acquisition brings new challenges. But I can't keep growing if I'm not helping others grow too."

The Gray Hat finally spoke, his voice quiet but clear. "The measure of a leader isn't what they accomplish alone. It's what continues after they're gone."

He stood, stretching casually. "Do you think these ducks migrate, or just stay put all winter?" Without waiting for an answer, he wandered toward the path leading back to the parking lot.

Priya shook her head, watching him go. "Does he ever give a straight answer?"

"No," Maya laughed. "But he's usually right." She turned to face her friend. "So what do you think? Ready for the next challenge?"

Priya's expression shifted from uncertainty to determination. "You know what? I think I am."

The morning sun broke through the clouds, casting long shadows across the pond. Something was ending, Maya realized, but something greater was beginning.

* * *

They reached the gravel parking lot, their footsteps crunching in sync. The morning had warmed slightly, but Maya could still see her breath forming little clouds as she spoke.

"I guess this session is over?" Priya asked, fishing her keys from her coat pocket.

The Gray Hat paused, his expression unreadable beneath his beard. "Oh, my troops always loved it when I acknowledged their good work. Here, you've earned this."

He extended his hand to Priya. Maya watched as they shook, but something passed between them, a small, metallic object pressed into Priya's palm. When they broke the handshake, the Gray Hat offered a goofy little salute, his fingers not quite touching his eyebrow.

Priya opened her hand to reveal a challenge coin. She turned it over, examining the intricate design and lettering on both sides. Her eyes widened.

"Wait, you were in the military?"

The Gray Hat didn't acknowledge the question. Instead, he turned to Maya, his demeanor shifting subtly.

"Belgium," he said simply. "Next month."

Maya blinked. "Belgium?"

"Brussels. NATO is hosting a summit on collective cybersecurity standards. They're looking for leaders who understand how to build influence across organizational boundaries." He leaned against his car, an understated sedan that somehow matched his personality perfectly. "The board has already approved it. Elena thinks it's a good opportunity."

Maya stared at him. "You talked to my CEO before asking me?"

"I didn't ask her," he said with a slight smile. "I told her you'd be perfect for it. She agreed."

Priya laughed. "And people think I'm direct."

The Gray Hat's eyes crinkled at the corners. "You know what we've been doing these past months, Maya? Building a framework for influence. But influence isn't just about individual tactics, it's about creating environments where security becomes the natural choice."

He gestured toward the pond they'd just left. "Designing for behavior shapes individual actions, but building culture shapes collective norms. That's what they need in Brussels: someone who understands that security isn't just about controls and compliance. It's about creating shared values that transcend organizational boundaries."

Maya felt a familiar mixture of irritation and respect. "You could have just asked me."

"I could have," he agreed. "But would you have said yes?"

She thought about it. "Probably not. I would have said I'm too busy."

"Exactly. Sometimes the people who need to lead don't see themselves as leaders." He opened his car door. "Just like the people who need to listen don't always see themselves as listeners."

Priya glanced at her watch. "I should get going. I've got a meeting with Ricky at ten to talk details." She turned to Maya. "Thank you. For everything."

They hugged briefly, and Priya climbed into her car.

The Gray Hat watched her drive away before turning back to Maya. "She'll do well."

"I know," Maya said. "That's why I recommended her."

"And you'll do well in Brussels."

Maya sighed, already mentally rearranging her calendar. "I haven't said yes yet."

The Gray Hat smiled. "You haven't said no, either." He slid into his car and started the engine. Through the open window, he added, "The greatest security leaders don't just protect systems, Maya. They transform cultures. Remember that when you're sitting at that table in Brussels."

As he drove away, Maya stood in the empty parking lot, thinking about how far they'd come and how much further there was to go.

Chapter 12:

Build a Security Culture, Not Just Awareness

Maya settled into her first-class seat, still bewildered by the entire situation. The plush leather cradled her body as she accepted a flute of champagne from the flight attendant.

"Anything else I can get for you, Ms. Tran?" the attendant asked.

"No, thank you. This is... perfect." Maya took a sip, savoring the crisp bubbles. Perfect and completely unexpected.

She'd spent the week preparing for Brussels, reading briefing documents and researching NATO's cybersecurity initiatives. The whole time, she kept waiting for someone to call and say there'd been a mistake. Security leaders at her level didn't typically get sent to international summits in first class. Yet here she was, 35,000 feet over the Atlantic, her seat transforming into a bed at the touch of a button.

Somewhere over Iceland, Maya noticed movement in her peripheral vision. A tall man with salt-and-pepper hair rose from his seat several rows ahead and made his way toward the restroom. Something about his bearing, shoulders back, chin slightly elevated, triggered her memory.

She'd seen that face before, but where? The man passed by, and recognition hit her. That stern profile, the ramrod-straight posture.

General Karim.

Maya nearly choked on her champagne. She'd never met him personally, but Priya had a framed photo with him in her office. Her former commanding officer. Priya quoted him constantly, wielding his wisdom like tactical weapons in meetings.

"Culture eats policy for breakfast," she'd say when someone proposed another security rule that would just be circumvented.

There was another one Maya had always found compelling, something about culture determining what happens when no one is watching. That resonated with her deeply. Security wasn't just about controls and monitoring; it was about what people chose to do when they thought no one would know.

Was Karim headed to the same summit? It seemed too coincidental. Maya wondered if she should introduce herself when he returned to his seat. "Hi, I work with Priya Desai" seemed like a good opener.

She smiled to herself. Maybe this wasn't just a random assignment. Maybe the Gray Hat had pulled more strings than she realized. Serendipity or orchestration? Either way, she suddenly felt like this summit might be more significant than she'd anticipated.

* * *

Maya stepped out of the sleek Uber Black into the evening air of Brussels. The hotel lobby gleamed with polished marble and crystal chandeliers, a world away from her usual business accommodations. After checking in and dropping her bags in a room that felt more like a luxury apartment than a hotel suite, her stomach reminded her she hadn't eaten since the light meal on the plane.

She wandered down to the hotel bar, a warm space with dark wood and leather seating. The bartender smiled as she approached, but Maya hesitated, scanning the unfamiliar Belgian beer options.

"Liam, get this nice woman the Westmalle Dubbel."

Maya turned to find General Karim sliding onto the stool beside her, his presence commanding even in civilian clothes.

"I... thank you," Maya managed, surprised by the intervention.

The bartender nodded and poured a rich amber liquid into a branded chalice. Maya took a tentative sip, and her eyes widened. The complex flavors, caramel, fruit, and a hint of spice, were unlike any beer she'd tasted before.

"This is incredible," she said, taking another sip.

"Belgian Trappist ale. Made by monks who've perfected the craft over centuries." Karim smiled. "I'm Samuel Karim."

"Maya Tran. I actually know who you are, sir. I work with Priya Desai at TechForward. She speaks very highly of you."

The general's face lit up. "Chief was one of the greatest cyber operators I've ever known. How is she these days? I haven't caught up with her much since she retired and moved to the big city."

"She's running our SOC, terrorizing analysts, and quoting you regularly. Especially about culture eating policy for breakfast."

Karim laughed. "That sounds like her. Though I believe I stole that line from Peter Drucker."

They fell into easy conversation, with Maya sharing stories about Priya's leadership style and the general offering anecdotes from their military days.

"So what brings you to Belgium, Ms. Tran?" he finally asked.

"The NATO summit. Though honestly, I'm still not entirely sure why I was selected." Maya described the strange circumstances, the last-minute invitation, the first-class ticket, and the luxurious accommodations.

"Actually, I had the strangest encounter in our parking lot last week. A man who sometimes wears a unicorn onesie gave me cryptic advice about the summit."

Karim nearly choked on his beer. "A unicorn onesie? Let me guess, he said something vague and philosophical, then disappeared?"

"Exactly! How did you know?"

"LT never really learned to be elegant or loquacious."

"LT? Like, lieutenant?"

"Ya, sounds like you're describing my cute little platoon leader, Lieutenant Callahan. I know he retired as a colonel from The Fort, but to me, he'll always be LT." Karim's eyes crinkled with amusement. "He got in so much trouble, but kept me out of a bunch when I was just a wee company commander."

Maya's mind raced. "The Gray Hat is... Callahan? And you know him?"

"He usually comes to these summits, but I didn't see him on the plane. He says he doesn't even have to buy plane tickets because he just has the miles to get a first-class ticket."

The realization hit Maya like a wave. The Gray Hat hadn't just recommended her for the summit, he'd given her his own ticket.

"What exactly is this summit about?" Maya asked, suddenly suspicious that there was more to it than she'd been briefed.

"This year's focus is actually something I think you'll find fascinating: security culture. Not just awareness, but how culture is shaped by observed behaviors and expectations." Karim leaned forward. "You can give people all the information in the world, but what they do when no one's watching, that's culture. And that's what truly protects organizations."

Maya felt a strange sense of alignment, as if invisible threads were connecting her recent experiences. "That's exactly what I've been working on at TechForward."

"Then perhaps," Karim said with a knowing smile, "you're exactly where you're supposed to be."

* * *

The next morning, Maya found herself in a sunlit conference room that overlooked the ancient streets of Brussels. She'd expected rows of chairs facing a podium, perhaps a PowerPoint presentation with bullet points on security awareness best practices. Instead, she discovered round tables arranged throughout the space, each with a small placard indicating discussion topics.

A silver-haired woman in a tailored navy suit approached. "Ms. Tran? I'm Admiral Winters. We're delighted you could join us." She gestured to a table near the window. "You'll be at table four, cultural transformation strategies."

Maya blinked. "I'm sorry, I think there might be a misunderstanding. I'm here to learn from the experts, not."

"Oh, we're all here to learn from each other," Admiral Winters said with a warm smile. "The Gray Hat spoke quite highly of your work at TechForward."

Before Maya could respond, the admiral moved on to greet other attendees. Maya made her way to table four, where she found herself seated between a Norwegian intelligence director and a British brigadier general. Across from her sat a woman whose name badge identified her as the CISO of a major European banking group.

The facilitator began with introductions, and Maya's stomach tightened as her turn approached. These people had decades of experience protecting national secrets and critical infrastructure. What could she possibly contribute?

"Maya Tran, CISO at TechForward," she said simply when her turn came.

"Ah, the gh05t5c1pt approach," said the brigadier, his eyes lighting with recognition. "I've followed your work on LinkedIn. Brilliant insights."

Maya felt heat rise to her face. This was the first time someone had referenced her online persona and seemed to know so much about her. And it was someone as prestigious as the brigadier.

"I, thank you," she managed.

As the discussion began, Maya remained quiet at first, listening to strategies employed by military and intelligence organizations. They spoke of training regimens, compliance requirements, and awareness campaigns.

When there was a natural pause, the facilitator turned to her. "Maya, you've been implementing some innovative approaches at TechForward. Would you share your perspective?"

All eyes turned to her, and Maya took a deep breath.

"We've shifted our focus from teaching security to removing barriers and changing defaults," she began, her voice growing stronger as she continued. "Traditional awareness programs assume people make bad security decisions because they don't know better. But in my experience, they usually know, they just choose convenience over security when the secure option is difficult."

She described her tiger team's work to redesign authentication flows, how they'd simplified incident reporting to eliminate blame, and their campaign to make secure file sharing easier than insecure alternatives.

"We measure success not by quiz scores but by behavior changes. Are people choosing secure options when no one's watching? That's culture, not just awareness."

To her surprise, the table leaned in. The Norwegian intelligence director asked detailed questions about implementation. The brigadier took notes. The banking CISO shared similar challenges she'd faced.

"In the military, this sometimes feels obvious," the brigadier said. "The stakes are clear; lives depend on security. But you've managed to create that same sense of purpose in a corporate environment."

Maya thought of the recent intelligence leak through Signal messages sent to the wrong recipients by high-ranking officials.

"Even with clear stakes, we're all human," she observed. "Culture isn't about perfect compliance, it's about creating an environment where secure behavior becomes the natural choice."

As the discussion continued, Maya realized she wasn't just a participant; she was a valued contributor. The Gray Hat hadn't sent her here just to learn. He'd sent her here to teach.

As the morning session wrapped up, the facilitator announced, "We'll reconvene after lunch to prepare presentations for tomorrow's plenary session. Each table will have fifteen minutes to share your cultural transformation strategies."

Maya's stomach dropped. The pit that had been forming all morning suddenly felt like a chasm. She'd come to Brussels expecting to sit quietly in the back row, take notes, and maybe ask a thoughtful question or two. Not present to NATO cybersecurity leaders and intelligence officials.

"I should have done more research before accepting this invitation," she muttered, pulling out her phone to frantically search for information about the summit while the others gathered their things.

The Norwegian intelligence director paused beside her. "First time at one of these?"

"That obvious?" Maya grimaced.

"Only to someone who's been there." He smiled. "The Gray Hat doesn't extend invitations lightly. You belong here."

Maya nodded, but the reassurance did little to settle her nerves. She spent lunch picking at her salad, reviewing her mental inventory of what she could possibly contribute to a formal presentation.

When they returned to their table, the brigadier general took charge naturally. "Right then, what's our approach? I suggest we focus on metrics and measurement, it seems we all had interesting perspectives there."

The banking CISO nodded. "Maya, your dashboards sounded fascinating. Could you elaborate?"

Maya pulled out her tablet and opened her presentation folder. "I've found that tracking behavioral indicators provides a much truer picture of security culture than traditional metrics." She turned the screen so everyone could see the clean, simple visualizations.

"Wait," the brigadier interrupted, brow furrowed. "You don't track open vulnerabilities and SOC alerts?"

"Oh, I do," Maya replied, swiping to a different screen. "But that's not what we show leadership or the rest of the organization. They don't care about that stuff."

She watched as understanding dawned across their faces, followed by nods of agreement.

"What they care about is whether people are actually using the secure tools we provide. Are they enabling MFA voluntarily? How many employees spot and report our internal phishing tests? How quickly do teams remediate when given options rather than mandates?"

The Norwegian leaned forward. "You're measuring choice, not compliance."

"Exactly." Maya felt her confidence building. "Compliance tells you if people follow rules when they know they're being watched. Choice tells you what they do when no one's looking."

For the next hour, they crafted their presentation, with each member contributing insights from their respective domains. The banking CISO shared her framework for incentivizing secure behavior without creating perverse incentives. The brigadier described how his unit had redesigned training to focus on team responsibility rather than individual blame.

As they worked, Maya found herself not just participating but often leading the discussion. These people, legends in their fields, were taking notes on her approaches, asking for her slide templates, requesting her GitHub handle.

A strange realization settled over her: she wasn't just a fortunate security architect in a single organization. She might actually be a thought leader.

She cringed internally at the term. Thought leader. It conjured images of LinkedIn influencers posting inspirational quotes over sunset backgrounds, desperately collecting followers and engagement metrics.

That wasn't her. She'd never sought the spotlight. She'd just tried to solve problems effectively, to make security work for people rather than against them.

But as the admiral stopped by their table to check progress and nodded approvingly at Maya's dashboard designs, she had to admit, these people genuinely wanted to hear what she had to say. Not because she was chasing attention, but because her approaches worked.

* * *

Maya blinked, momentarily disoriented by the moderator's question. The man, she thought he'd introduced himself as a field marshal, though she wasn't entirely clear on military hierarchies, leaned forward expectantly.

"What made it real to you? When did you know that it was actually working?"

She hesitated, organizing her thoughts. The fluorescent lights of the conference room buzzed overhead as the weight of all those decorated uniforms and impressive titles pressed in around her.

The brigadier, Williamson, she remembered, caught her eye with a knowing look. "Would you share with us, gh05t5c1pt?"

Maya nearly choked. Her online handle. Here. In this room full of military brass and intelligence officials. The Norwegian's eyes widened slightly in recognition, and the banking CISO gave a small nod of respect.

"I... how did you, "

"Game recognizes game, as they say," Williamson said, his British accent clipping the words precisely. "Brilliant work. We've implemented some of your ideas across several NATO operations."

The field marshal, or whatever he was, looked confused. "gh05t5c1pt?"

"A handle, sir," Williamson explained. "Rather well-known in certain circles."

Maya took a deep breath. This was surreal. She watched the pilot across the table, making those strange hand gestures as he whispered something to the person next to him. What was it with pilots and talking with their hands?

She refocused on the original question.

"When did I know it was working?" Maya straightened her posture. "It wasn't a big security win or an executive presentation. It was something small but meaningful."

The room quieted.

"We had a customer support representative named Jenna. Not technical, not security-focused. Just someone trying to do her job well. One day, she received an urgent email supposedly from our CEO asking for gift card purchases for client appreciation."

Maya noticed the knowing nods around the table. Classic scam.

"But instead of just following procedure, Jenna did something unexpected. She created a separate, secure channel to verify the request, not because she'd been trained specifically on that scenario, but because we'd built a culture where verification had become second nature."

The Norwegian intelligence director leaned forward. "And this was significant because?"

"Because she didn't follow a rule, she applied a principle," Maya explained. "When I asked her afterward why she didn't just report it through our phishing button, she said something I'll never forget: 'I knew it was probably fake, but I wanted to make sure we didn't miss a real opportunity if it wasn't. I figured verifying was the best way to protect both our customers and the company.'"

Maya smiled at the memory. "She wasn't thinking about security as a separate thing. She was thinking about protection as part of her job."

"And that's when you knew," the banking CISO said quietly.

"Yes. When security became invisible, when it was just part of how people approached their work rather than an extra step or consideration, that's when I knew we'd succeeded."

The pilot, "Spanky," someone had called him, though Maya couldn't imagine using such a nickname with a straight face, finally stopped gesturing and nodded thoughtfully.

"Culture eats compliance for breakfast," he said.

"Exactly," Maya replied. "You can force people to follow security rules when they're being watched. But culture is what they do when no one's looking, when they have to make quick decisions with imperfect information."

The field marshal wrote something in his notebook. "And how did you measure that shift?"

"That's the interesting part," Maya said, warming to the subject. "We started tracking decisions, not just actions. Not 'did you report the phish?' but 'what did you consider before deciding what to do?'"

As she continued explaining, Maya realized she'd stopped feeling like an impostor. These people weren't intimidating anymore. They were just colleagues facing the same fundamental challenge: how to make security matter to people who had other priorities.

* * *

Maya still couldn't believe this was happening. She'd spent the night before trying some of the local beers at the reception, more varieties in one place than she'd ever seen back home. She might actually become a beer drinker if she had access to brews like these instead of the watery stuff that passed for beer in most American bars.

"So, how do you actually build this culture?" The Norwegian intelligence director's question pulled her back to the present. "Beyond waiting for moments like your customer service example."

Maya nodded, gathering her thoughts. "You can't mandate culture, but you can nurture it. We found three approaches that consistently worked."

She stood and moved to the whiteboard, uncapping a marker with

STORIES

STORIES　　**RECOGNITION**　　**FEEDBACK LOOPS**

practiced ease. The military and intelligence professionals watched with focused attention as she wrote "STORIES" in bold letters.

"First, we collected and shared stories of good security decisions, not just breaches averted, but business enabled safely. We created short video testimonials from staff about times they'd made security-conscious choices and how it helped the company."

She drew a simple stick figure with a speech bubble. "These weren't polished productions, just thirty-second clips recorded on phones. But they normalized the behavior we wanted and created peer models."

The banking CISO nodded. "Social proof."

"Exactly." Maya wrote "RECOGNITION" next. "Second, we made security achievements visible. Not with meaningless certificates, but through tangible recognition."

She described their "Security MVP" program, where anyone could nominate colleagues who'd made security-conscious decisions. Winners received not just acknowledgment but a small budget to spend on their team.

"The key was making it peer-driven, not top-down. When your colleagues recognize your security mindset, it matters more than when your CISO does."

The pilot, Spanky, raised an eyebrow. "How'd you measure effectiveness?"

"That's the third approach." Maya wrote "FEEDBACK LOOPS" on the board. "We created real-time feedback mechanisms that showed people the impact of their actions."

She explained how they'd built simple dashboards showing how security behaviors affected business metrics. When teams reduced their risk scores, they could see corresponding improvements in customer trust ratings and sales cycle times.

"People need to see that their efforts matter. Abstract 'risk reduction' doesn't motivate anyone. But showing a team that their improved security practices directly correlated with faster sales cycles? That got attention."

Williamson, the brigadier, tapped his pen thoughtfully against his notepad. "Did you encounter resistance?"

"Constantly." Maya smiled. "Our biggest breakthrough came when we stopped treating resistance as an obstacle and started treating it as feedback."

She described how they'd invited the most vocal skeptics to join their security culture working group. "We didn't try to convert them, we asked them to help us understand what wasn't working."

The field marshal leaned forward. "And?"

"And most of them became our strongest advocates once they felt heard. They didn't resist security, they resisted being controlled without context."

As Maya continued explaining their approach, she felt a calm confidence she hadn't expected in this room. These weren't just military and intelligence leaders; they were people facing the same fundamental challenge she'd tackled: how to make security matter to those with different priorities.

"The most powerful culture-building technique," she concluded, "isn't a technique at all. It's authenticity. When people see security leaders genuinely trying to understand their world instead of forcing them to comply with ours, that's when culture starts to shift."

* * *

When does this stop feeling surreal, Maya wondered as she took another sip of her dark Belgian beer. Across the dimly lit hotel bar, Colonel Deveraux, a military strategist whose work she'd read in graduate school, was animatedly explaining her presentation to a Finnish intelligence director.

"What Tran understands, and what most security practitioners miss, is that culture creates the conditions where good decisions happen naturally," Deveraux said, sketching something on a napkin. "It's why her approach scales when compliance-based models collapse under their own weight."

Maya still couldn't process that these people knew who she was. Yesterday, a German cybersecurity director approached her after her talk, tablet in hand, to show her a GitHub repository.

"You're gh05t5c1pt, yes?" he'd asked quietly, a conspiratorial smile on his face. "Your IAM automation scripts saved my team months of work last year."

She'd nearly choked on her coffee. Her online identity wasn't exactly a secret, but she'd never expected it to follow her into these circles.

"Tran!" The Norwegian intelligence director waved her over. "Come settle a debate. Deveraux thinks your feedback loop approach would work in classified environments. I'm skeptical."

As Maya walked over, she caught fragments of other conversations. An Australian was telling someone they planned to "take this straight to the committee when we get home." A British officer mentioned "briefing the palace security team."

The palace. As in, where the royal family lived. These weren't just ideas anymore; they were becoming doctrine.

"The beauty of Maya's model," Deveraux was saying as she approached, "is that it acknowledges human nature instead of fighting it. People will always choose convenience over security unless security becomes the convenient choice."

"Or unless the culture makes secure behavior the expected norm," Maya added, sliding into an empty chair.

The Norwegian nodded appreciatively. "The question is implementation. My analysts operate in compartmentalized environments. Your feedback mechanisms would cross classification boundaries."

Maya considered this. "The principle remains valid even if the implementation differs. The core question is: how do people know their security actions matter? In classified environments, you might need proxy metrics or delayed feedback, but people still need to see impact."

A woman Maya recognized as Denmark's deputy cyber commander joined them. "I've been thinking about your recognition model since this morning. We're implementing something similar next quarter."

The conversation flowed for another hour, with Maya fielding questions she never imagined answering. These weren't theoretical discussions; these people controlled national security infrastructures and were treating her ideas as operational blueprints.

Later, as the bar began to empty, Deveraux lingered. "You know, when they added you to the speaker list, there was skepticism. Another corporate CISO with PowerPoint platitudes." He smiled. "You've changed minds this week."

"Including yours?" Maya asked.

"I recognized your handle from some Signal groups. Knew you'd be worth listening to." He finished his beer. "What you've built at TechForward isn't just a security program. It's a template."

As Maya walked back to her room, her phone buzzed with a calendar invite. The subject line read: "UN Cybersecurity Working Group - Guest Speaker Request."

She stopped in the empty hallway, staring at her phone. When had this become her life? Six months ago, she'd been fighting for budget scraps and explaining basic risk concepts to executives. Now her framework was being discussed in palaces and parliaments.

The surreal feeling wasn't fading. Maybe it wasn't supposed to. Maybe this was what happened when you built something that resonated beyond your own walls; it stopped being just yours and became something larger.

Maya accepted the calendar invite and continued down the hallway, wondering what Priya would say when she told her their SOC practices might soon influence international security doctrine.

* * *

Maya stared at the UN invitation a moment longer, then jumped as her phone buzzed again. A text notification slid down from the top of her screen.

It was him. The Gray Hat. Somehow always appearing exactly when her mind was spinning fastest.

"Remember, they're all just people. They all have to eat food. They all have to use the bathroom. I'm hearing good things. I'm also hearing that your eyes are ginormous. Breathe. Breathe."

Maya couldn't help but laugh. Her shoulders relaxed as she leaned against the hallway wall.

Who was this guy, really? Was he actually this zen all the time, or was it just an elaborate persona? She remembered the time he'd shown up to a critical vendor security review in that ridiculous pink unicorn onesie yet somehow commanded the room more effectively than anyone in formal attire.

Her phone buzzed again.

170

"Where does culture begin?"

Maya's fingers hovered over the keyboard. She knew this answer; they'd discussed it during their third meeting, when she was struggling to get buy-in from the engineering team. Culture shapes the organization; leadership, in turn, shapes the culture.

She typed her response, then paused before sending. The hallway was empty except for the soft hum of the air conditioning. Six months ago, she'd been drowning in alerts and fighting for basic visibility. Now, people were implementing her frameworks in classified environments and royal residences.

Her phone buzzed once more before she could reply.

"You don't need to answer me. You already know. You've always known. That's why they're listening."

Maya smiled and pushed off from the wall, continuing toward her room. The Gray Hat was right. They were just people, smart, powerful people, but people, nonetheless. And people responded to authenticity, to frameworks that acknowledged human nature instead of fighting it.

She texted back: "Thanks. For everything."

Three dots appeared, then: "The unicorn onesie says you're welcome. Get some sleep. Tomorrow, you get to be both gh05t5c1pt AND Maya Tran. That's twice the power."

Maya laughed out loud this time. Maybe someday she'd figure out how he always knew exactly what she needed to hear.

Chapter 13:

Lead Through Clarity,

Not Authority

Spring had come fast to Singapore, though Maya wasn't sure if seasons truly existed here. The perpetual warmth and humidity made it feel like an eternal summer, broken only by monsoon rains that washed the city clean. Maya didn't mind at all. After years of East Coast winters, the consistent warmth felt like a blessing.

She adjusted her blazer and checked her reflection in the hotel mirror. Her hair was pulled back in a sleek bun, professional yet comfortable in the tropical climate. Six months since leaving TechForward, and sometimes she still reached for an employee badge that was no longer there.

The VC firm that worked with the Gray Hat approached her the week after Brussels. Their offer was unexpected but intriguing: become a full-time consultant, helping organizations transform their security posture using her frameworks. The role meant freedom, impact, and a chance to spread what she'd built beyond a single company's walls.

"The Johnny Appleseed of cybersecurity leadership," the Gray Hat had called her when she'd accepted the position. The nickname had stuck.

Maya gathered her materials and headed down to the lobby. Her client this week was a global banking institution with offices overlooking Marina Bay. Their security team was technically impressive, with state-of-the-art tools, a substantial budget, and skilled analysts. Yet something was missing, and the CISO had brought her in to identify the gap.

The morning air was already thick with humidity as Maya's taxi wove through Singapore's immaculate streets. Glass towers reflected the sunrise, their windows glinting like scales on some massive creature awakening for the day. Maya reviewed her notes one last time before arriving at the bank's headquarters.

"Ms. Tran, welcome." The security director greeted her with a firm handshake. "We're looking forward to your insights."

Throughout the morning, Maya observed their operations with practiced eyes. Their SOC was a marvel of efficiency, alerts categorized, threats hunted, vulnerabilities patched. The team moved with precision, their processes clearly documented and followed.

Yet as she sat in on meetings and watched interactions, she identified what was missing. The security team operated as a perfect machine, but in isolation. When product managers entered the room, conversations grew stilted. When engineers joined calls, subtle tensions emerged. Security was respected but separate, a function apart from the business rather than integrated within it.

During a break, Maya stepped out onto the building's observation deck. Singapore sprawled before her, a testament to intentional design. Nothing in this city happened by accident; every tree, every building, every road was carefully planned to create a harmonious whole.

Her phone buzzed with a text from the Gray Hat: "Clarity influences more than position."

Maya smiled. After all this time, he still knew exactly what she was thinking. The bank's security team had authority but lacked clarity, specifically the ability to translate technical truths into business language, making complex concepts accessible without diluting their importance.

In the afternoon session with the bank's leadership team, Maya didn't discuss technical controls or compliance frameworks. Instead, she focused on communication patterns and decision flows.

"Your security is technically sound," she explained, "but isolated. The strongest security programs don't just protect the business, they enable it. That requires a different kind of leadership."

The CISO leaned forward. "What kind?"

"Leadership through clarity, not authority," Maya replied. "Your team has the positional power to enforce security, but they're missing the translational skills to make security matter to others."

She outlined a transformation plan that prioritized communication pathways over new tools, relationship-building over additional controls. The executives exchanged glances. This wasn't the technical assessment they'd expected.

"This approach transformed TechForward's security posture," Maya continued. "Not by adding more technology, but by changing how security was understood and valued across the organization."

"I need more examples," the bank's CISO said, leaning forward with interest. His skepticism had softened, but Maya could see he wasn't fully convinced. "This sounds compelling in theory, but how does it actually play out in practice?"

Maya nodded, understanding his need for concrete illustrations. She'd encountered this reaction countless times since starting her consulting work, security leaders intellectually grasped the concept of clarity over authority, but struggled to envision its implementation.

"Let me share something fundamental," she said, setting her tablet aside. "Clarity creates commitment while authority only creates compliance. And there's a world of difference between the two."

The executives exchanged glances as Maya continued.

"When you lead through authority, people follow your security directives because they have to. They check the boxes, implement the controls, and attend the training. But the moment you're not looking, they find workarounds. The security measures become obstacles to overcome rather than protections to value."

The CISO nodded slowly. "We see that with our password policies. Everyone follows them, but then they write them on sticky notes."

"Exactly. That's compliance without commitment," Maya said. "But when you lead through clarity, when you help people truly understand the 'why' behind security measures and connect them to what they already care about, they become advocates rather than reluctant participants."

Maya paused, thinking of the perfect example. "Let me tell you about something I heard in Brussels last month. This comes from a military context, but the principle is universal."

She leaned forward, her voice taking on a storyteller's cadence. "A naval intelligence unit was struggling with classified information handling. Despite strict protocols and severe penalties for violations, they continued to find classified documents left unsecured. More training, more reminders, more spot checks, nothing worked."

The room grew quiet as executives were drawn into the narrative.

"Their new commander took a different approach. Instead of doubling down on authority, she focused on clarity. She brought in actual intelligence analysts who used the unit's reports and had them explain exactly how those reports influenced critical missions. They shared specific examples of how seemingly minor details had saved lives."

Maya gestured with her hands as she continued. "She didn't change a single policy or procedure. What she changed was understanding. Suddenly, those classified documents weren't abstract requirements to be followed; they were vital links in a chain that protected real people."

"And the violations stopped?" the CFO asked.

"Not immediately, but they dropped by over eighty percent in three months. When they did find violations, team members were often the ones reporting them, not hiding them."

Maya leaned back in her chair. "The commander didn't need more authority; she already had plenty. What she needed was to create clarity about why the security measures mattered in terms her team already valued."

The CISO nodded thoughtfully. "So instead of telling our development teams they need to implement encryption because it's required, we should help them understand how it protects the customers they're trying to serve."

"Precisely," Maya smiled. "Authority can force action, but only clarity can change minds. And changed minds drive sustainable security in ways that authority never can."

The executives exchanged glances, and Maya could see the shift in their expressions. They weren't just hearing her words; they were beginning to envision how this approach might transform their own security culture.

"The beauty of leading through clarity," Maya concluded, "is that it turns security from something people have to do into something they want to do. And that's when security truly becomes part of your organizational DNA."

* * *

"Speaking of clarity during high-pressure situations," Maya said, her voice softening as she recalled a memory, "I experienced this firsthand during my time at Meridian Health."

She hadn't planned to share this story, but something in the CISO's expression, a mixture of intellectual understanding and practical doubt, made her realize that a personal example might bridge the gap.

"We had a major security incident three years ago. A sophisticated threat actor had gained access to our network, and we discovered indicators of compromise in our patient billing systems."

Maya remembered the moment with perfect clarity, the flashing alerts, the flood of adrenaline, the team's faces tight with panic as they gathered in the war room.

"Our team was excellent technically, but as the pressure mounted, people started working in silos. Engineers were implementing containment measures without coordinating. Analysts were chasing different leads without sharing findings. Leadership was demanding updates every fifteen minutes."

She paused, remembering how she'd felt the room's energy spiraling toward chaos.

"I could have asserted authority, started barking orders, assigned tasks, and demanded reports. That might have created structure, but not understanding."

The executives leaned forward, fully engaged now.

"Instead, I took ten minutes to create clarity. I drew our network architecture on the whiteboard, marked what we knew about the compromise, and outlined three clear priorities: contain the active threat, preserve evidence, and maintain critical patient services."

Maya smiled slightly at the memory. "I didn't tell people what to do. I helped them understand what we were facing and why certain actions were more important than others. Once they understood the landscape and priorities, they organized themselves more effectively than I could have directed them."

The CISO nodded slowly. "And the outcome?"

"We contained the breach within four hours. No patient data was exfiltrated. And most importantly, the team functioned as a cohesive unit throughout the response."

Maya tapped her fingers lightly on the table. "What struck me afterward was the feedback. Team members didn't talk about my leadership or decisions. They talked about how clearly they understood what we were facing and why each action mattered."

She met each executive's eyes in turn. "That's the difference. When you lead through authority, people remember your commands. When you lead through clarity, they remember their own understanding. And understanding drives behavior long after the crisis ends."

* * *

Maya noticed a young woman at the end of the table. She hadn't spoken during the entire presentation, but her eyes followed every gesture, every slide transition with intense focus. Her business attire seemed slightly too formal compared to the other executives, a telltale sign of someone young trying to project authority in a room where they felt outranked.

"Any other questions?" Maya asked, making deliberate eye contact with the young woman.

The executive hesitated, then straightened her shoulders. "I understand the concept, but I'm struggling to see how this works in practice. Authority gives clear direction in crisis situations. Clarity seems... subjective."

Maya recognized the skepticism. It was the same doubt she'd harbored early in her career when the Gray Hat first challenged her command-and-control instincts.

"That's an excellent question," Maya said, appreciating the woman's candor. "May I ask your role here at the bank?"

"Leila Zhang. I lead the application security team." Her voice carried a quiet confidence despite her youth. "We're responsible for securing the new mobile banking platform."

Maya nodded, recognizing an opportunity. "I'm reminded of a colleague who faced a similar challenge. James Chen was CISO at Keystone when I worked with them during a merger. Brilliant technical mind, but he struggled with getting teams to implement security requirements."

The executives perked up at the familiar company name.

"James had authority, plenty of it. As CISO, he could mandate controls and escalate non-compliance. But his technical brilliance actually created a barrier. His explanations were accurate but impenetrable to non-security teams."

Maya moved closer to Leila's end of the table. "The turning point came during a critical vulnerability in their payment processing system. Rather than issuing technical directives, James created visual maps showing exactly how customer data moved through each component, where the vulnerability existed, and which specific transactions were at risk."

"Instead of saying 'implement input validation to prevent SQL injection,' he showed how a specific transaction type could be manipulated to extract customer account details. He translated the technical risk into business impact with crystal clarity."

Maya watched as understanding dawned in Leila's eyes.

"The development team implemented fixes in record time, not because James ordered them to, but because they clearly understood what was at stake. More importantly, they started proactively consulting him on new features, bringing him designs before writing code."

"So it wasn't that he stopped being technical," Leila said slowly.

"Exactly. He remained technically brilliant but learned to translate that expertise into language that created shared understanding. His influence expanded far beyond his authority because people acted on their own understanding, not just his directives."

Maya glanced around the room, seeing the executives nodding. "When you lead through clarity, you create understanding that persists even when you're not in the room. That's not subjective, it's actually more reliable than authority, which only works when someone's watching."

Leila nodded thoughtfully, jotting something in her notebook.

"The most powerful security leaders I've worked with," Maya concluded, "don't just know the right answers; they help others discover why those answers matter. They don't diminish their technical expertise; they amplify its impact by making it accessible to everyone who needs to act on it."

* * *

Maya watched the afternoon sun cast long shadows across the restaurant's private dining room. Through the floor-to-ceiling windows, the city's financial district glittered below them, a fitting backdrop for their post-presentation dinner. She'd been pleasantly surprised when Dominic, the bank's CISO, extended the invitation.

"To clarity over authority," Dominic raised his glass in a toast. "And to Maya, for articulating what I've been trying to tell my leadership team for months."

The small group clinked glasses. Maya took a sip of her sparkling water, savoring the moment. These post-engagement dinners were rare opportunities to see the human side of security leadership, the personalities behind the policies.

"I've been thinking about your presentation all afternoon," Leila said, the young AppSec lead who had questioned Maya during the session. "It actually reminded me of something that happened here last month."

Maya leaned forward, intrigued. "Oh?"

"We had an incident with our customer data API," Leila explained, setting down her fork beside a half-eaten plate of perfectly seared scallops. "Nothing catastrophic, but concerning. Our standard protocol would have been for me or Dominic to lead the response."

Dominic nodded. "But we were both at the annual security conference in Vegas."

"Exactly," Leila continued. "So, this junior analyst, Raj, he's only been with us eight months, stepped up. No authority whatsoever, technically reports to my deputy."

Maya noticed how the entire table had quieted, everyone's attention drawn to Leila's story.

"Instead of panicking or waiting for instructions, Raj created this incredible visualization of the affected systems. He mapped out the data flows, highlighted the anomalies, and added timestamps of suspicious activities."

"He shared it with both the security team and the developers," added Chen, the infrastructure security director. "I remember opening that email and immediately understanding the situation. No technical jargon, just pure clarity."

Maya felt a flutter of satisfaction. Her words hadn't just been heard; they'd resonated enough for the team to connect them to their own experiences.

"The best part," Dominic said, "was that Raj didn't need to tell anyone what to do. Teams started coordinating on their own because the visualization made it obvious where the problems were and who needed to fix what."

"We contained the issue in three hours," Leila finished. "Normally, something like that would have taken us all day, with multiple status meetings and escalations."

The server arrived with their main courses, a parade of culinary artistry that momentarily diverted everyone's attention. Maya's sesame-crusted tuna was arranged like a jewel on the plate, surrounded by vibrant local vegetables she couldn't even name.

"The food here is incredible," Maya remarked, taking her first bite. The flavors were complex yet harmonious,with umami depth balanced by bright acidity.

"One of the perks of this city," Dominic smiled. "But to finish Raj's story, we actually created a new role for him after that incident. He's now leading our security visualization initiative."

"From junior analyst to program lead in eight months," Chen added. "Not because of tenure or technical certifications, but because he showed us a better way to communicate risk."

Maya nodded appreciatively. "That's exactly the point. Authority comes from a title, but influence comes from adding value in ways others recognize."

"To Raj," Leila raised her glass in another toast. "And to gh05t5c1pt."

Maya nearly choked on her tuna. "I'm sorry?"

"Your handle, right?" Leila's eyes sparkled. "I've been following your X account for years. Your insights on current events have helped shape my understanding of this field."

Maya felt heat rise to her cheeks. Her online persona was her private playground, a space where she could contribute purely on technical merit, without the baggage of titles or politics.

"How did you, "

"The way you explained the trust model earlier," Leila shrugged. "Same metaphors you used in your ReadMe documentation. Plus, you have a very distinctive way of diagramming access flows."

* * *

Leila's eyes danced with mischief. "I've been wondering when you'd realize I recognized you. Your code is like a signature – unmistakable."

Maya smiled, recovering her composure. "I'm flattered you'd connect the dots. Most people keep those worlds separate."

"That's what makes your approach so refreshing," Leila pressed. "You bridge technical excellence with practical communication. What else should we know about this strategy?"

Maya considered the question, setting down her fork. "The most powerful technique is simplification without oversimplification. Take complex security concepts and distill them to their essence."

"Like what you did with the threat modeling framework?" Dominic asked.

"Exactly. I replaced twenty pages of technical specifications with three questions: 'What are we building? What could go wrong? What are we doing about it?'" Maya gestured with her hands. "Security professionals often mistake complexity for thoroughness. But clarity requires the courage to simplify."

"Any other practical methods?" Chen leaned forward, genuinely curious.

"Visual thinking transforms abstract risks into tangible concerns," Maya explained. "When I need executives to understand a complex vulnerability, I sketch it rather than describe it. Our brains process visual information differently from text."

Leila nodded eagerly. "That's what Raj did with the incident visualization."

"And it worked brilliantly," Maya affirmed. "Another powerful technique is metaphor. When I explain zero-trust architecture, I don't discuss microsegmentation and least privilege. I talk about a museum where every exhibit has its own security guard checking credentials, rather than just one guard at the entrance."

"These all seem so... obvious," Chen mused. "Yet we rarely practice them."

"Because we're trained to value technical precision over human understanding," Maya replied. "But security that isn't understood isn't implemented. The most technically perfect solution fails if no one follows it."

As the conversation continued, Maya watched Leila taking notes on her phone. She recognized that hunger for practical wisdom – the same appetite she'd once had when listening to the Gray Hat's cryptic guidance. The circle was complete: once the student, now the teacher.

* * *

Maya felt a flutter of disbelief as the group articulated the very principles she'd spent years refining. Dominic summarized perfectly: "So clarity creates confidence, which influences decisions more effectively than authority ever could."

"Exactly," Chen added. "When people understand the 'why,' they make better decisions without supervision."

A warmth spread through Maya's chest that had nothing to do with the coffee in her hand. One year ago, she'd agonized over leaving her CISO position to become a consultant. The security field needed institutional change, not just another technical specialist. But this moment, watching her ideas take root in minds that would carry them to different organizations, validated that leap.

Leila tapped her notebook. "This approach scales beyond what any single security team could accomplish."

Maya nodded, suddenly overwhelmed by gratitude. Her work now touched organizations she'd never directly serve, through people like these who would implement these principles in their own contexts. The ripple effect stretched far beyond what she could have achieved in one company, no matter how influential her position there.

"Thank you for sharing this," she said quietly. "Seeing you connect with these ideas... it matters more than you know."

Maya returned to her hotel room, her mind still buzzing from the dinner conversation. She'd never expected her online identity to follow her to Singapore, but somehow it felt right. The walls between her professional and technical selves were thinning, creating a more integrated and powerful entity.

She kicked off her heels and pulled out her phone, scrolling to find Callahan's contact. Their text exchanges had become a ritual after each consulting engagement, with her sharing insights and him responding with cryptic wisdom that somehow always hit the mark.

"Singapore team gets it," she typed. "They connected clarity to influence faster than any group I've worked with. Leila even recognized my gh05t5c1pt work. That was unexpected."

She hit send and walked to the window, gazing at the city's spectacular skyline. The lights of Marina Bay Sands glowed against the night sky, a testament to human ambition and design.

Her phone buzzed moments later.

"Excellent. You're building ripples that will continue long after you leave. Brussels connections paying off?"

Maya smiled. Of course, he'd ask about that. The NATO summit had opened doors she'd never anticipated, creating a network of security leaders across continents.

"UN cybersecurity working group next month," she replied. "And the Singaporean bank wants me back to train their regional teams."

Three dots appeared, disappeared, then reappeared.

"I'll say this: clarity creates immediate impact; building capability creates a lasting legacy. Dominic mentioned you'll be working with their KL office next. Ricky's friend runs security there. Small world."

Maya shook her head, still amazed at how Callahan seemed to know everything before she told him. She was about to reply when another message appeared.

"What's next after Singapore?"

She paused, considering. What was next? Each engagement built on the previous one, expanding her influence in ways she couldn't have imagined a year ago.

"Tokyo," she typed. "Financial services consortium wants help building security communication frameworks across member organizations."

The response came quickly: "Perfect. You're ready."

Maya stared at those three words, feeling their weight. Ready for what? She had a feeling he knew something she didn't, as usual.

Tomorrow, she'd meet with the Malaysian team, planting more seeds that would grow long after she departed. The thought filled her with quiet satisfaction. This wasn't just about fixing security problems anymore. It was about creating capability that would outlast her presence.

She set her phone aside and began preparing for tomorrow, her mind already mapping out how to help the next team discover their own path to clarity.

Chapter 14:

Build a Legacy of Capability, Not Dependency

Maya stepped into the gleaming conference room in Tokyo's financial district, the city's skyline creating a dramatic backdrop through floor-to-ceiling windows. She arranged her materials with practiced efficiency, savoring these quiet moments before client meetings. The Mitsubishi Financial Group consortium represented her largest engagement yet, spanning seven organizations with varying security maturity.

Takahashi-san, the consortium coordinator, entered with his team. His formal bow contrasted with the worry lines etched around his eyes.

"Tran-san, welcome to Tokyo. We've heard remarkable things about your work in Singapore."

Maya returned the bow. "Thank you for the opportunity. I'm eager to understand your specific challenges."

Once settled, Takahashi-san didn't waste time with pleasantries. "Our security initiatives start strong but fade quickly when consultants leave. We implement recommendations, but nothing seems to stick. The moment external support ends, we revert to old patterns."

The other executives nodded in solemn agreement.

"You've identified a common pattern," Maya said, moving to the whiteboard. "Many organizations focus on implementing solutions rather than building capability."

She drew two simple diagrams, one showing all work flowing through a central figure, another showing distributed expertise with supporting connections.

CENTRALIZED EXPERTISE | DISTRIBUTED EXPERTISE

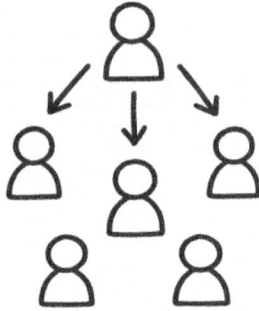

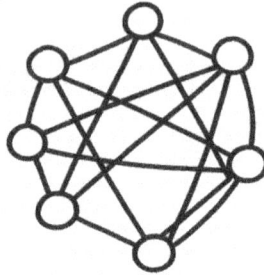

"Leadership isn't about being the security expert who approves everything," she explained, tapping the first diagram. "That creates a bottleneck where progress depends entirely on you. When you leave, everything stalls."

She moved to the second diagram. "True leadership builds organizational capability. Instead of being the bottleneck, you become the enabler."

Maya shared examples from her recent engagements, how a European bank transformed by shifting from approval-based processes to capability-building frameworks.

"The goal isn't perfect security implemented by you," she said. "It's developing your teams, so they make smart security decisions when you're not in the room."

Yamamoto, the CISO from one of the smaller banks, leaned forward. "This is exactly our problem. I personally review everything. Nothing moves without me, and I'm drowning."

"And when you're on vacation?" Maya asked gently.

"Nothing moves," he admitted. "Or worse, they make decisions without proper consideration."

Maya nodded. "Today, we'll map your current decision flows and identify where capability gaps exist. But first, I'd like to hear from each of you, what would success look like a year from now?"

As they began sharing their visions, Maya noticed Takahashi-san's expression shifting from concern to thoughtful consideration. The real work was just beginning.

* * *

"I'll share something I learned the hard way," Maya said, moving closer to Takahashi as the others broke into discussion groups. "My first leadership role, I wanted to prove my value. I became the approval checkpoint for everything security-related."

Takahashi nodded, recognition flickering across his face. "The security guardian."

"Exactly. My team couldn't move without me. Projects stalled waiting for my review." Maya sketched a simple funnel on her notepad. "I became this, the bottleneck. Everything poured in but only trickled out."

She watched Takahashi study the drawing, his shoulders tensing slightly.

"The irony is that while trying to reduce risk, I actually created a massive vulnerability, myself." She softened her tone, recognizing his discomfort. "If I got sick, went on vacation, or left the company, security decisions would either halt completely or bypass proper consideration."

Takahashi removed his glasses, rubbing the bridge of his nose. "This morning, three projects were delayed because I couldn't attend their security reviews yesterday."

Maya nodded, letting him reach his own conclusion rather than pushing her point.

"What changed for you?" he finally asked.

"I started measuring different things. Instead of tracking how many reviews I completed, I tracked how many decisions my team could make without me." She drew another diagram showing a distributed network. "I built decision frameworks, not approval processes."

She noticed Takahashi's gaze drift toward his team across the room, who were engaged in an animated discussion with her colleagues.

"Your team is full of capable people," Maya said gently. "They're just waiting for permission to apply their knowledge."

"But what if they make mistakes?"

"They will," Maya smiled. "Just as we did. But smaller mistakes caught early create less damage than major ones discovered too late. And each mistake becomes a learning opportunity."

Takahashi considered this, then asked, "How do you balance oversight with empowerment?"

"Clear guardrails, not gates. Define boundaries within which people can move freely, then focus your attention on decisions that truly need your experience." Maya sketched a final diagram. "Your most valuable contribution isn't making every decision, it's building a security ecosystem that functions whether you're present or not."

Takahashi studied the diagram, nodding slowly. "This is how we create something lasting."

"Exactly," Maya said. "Not dependency, but capability."

* * *

Maya sees an opportunity to pull in concepts from Lean, the four types of work, and workflow. Takahashi had made himself the constraint. Maya had done this exact thing before. Finally, she shifted from doing the work to developing her team's capabilities.

Maya noticed Takahashi glancing anxiously at his phone for the third time in ten minutes. His team was still engaged in their breakout discussions, but his attention kept drifting to the steady stream of notifications.

"Everything okay?" she asked quietly.

He sighed, setting the phone face down. "Three different teams are waiting on my security review. The mobile banking feature can't proceed without my sign-off, the threat modeling for the new payment gateway is stalled, and compliance needs my approval on vendor assessments."

Maya recognized the symptoms immediately. "You've become the constraint in your own process."

"The what?"

"In Lean thinking, there's always one part of any system that limits throughput, the constraint." Maya reached for a fresh sheet of paper. "Right now, that's you."

Takahashi's expression shifted from confusion to recognition. "I never thought of it that way."

187

"Let me share something that changed everything for me." Maya sketched a simple workflow diagram. "When I was at FinSecure, I categorized our security work into four distinct types. Business projects, things driving revenue. Internal improvements, making our own capabilities better. Change management, planned maintenance, and updates. And finally, unplanned work, the fires and emergencies."

She labeled each category on the diagram.

"Most security leaders drown because they try to handle all four types simultaneously, with the same urgency, through the same approval process." She tapped her pen on the paper. "Sound familiar?"

Takahashi nodded, his eyes fixed on the diagram.

"The breakthrough came when I realized different types of work need different flows," Maya added arrows showing separate pathways. "Business projects needed thorough review, but clear timelines. Internal improvements could be batched. Change management needs standard processes. And unplanned work needs rapid triage."

"But how did you maintain control?" Takahashi asked, the concern evident in his voice.

"I shifted from controlling decisions to shaping how decisions got made." Maya drew a new diagram showing a hub-and-spoke model. "I created decision frameworks for each type of work, trained my team to use them, and then gradually stepped back."

She described how she'd implemented WIP limits for each work category, visualized the flow on kanban boards, and created clear criteria for when escalation was truly needed.

"Instead of being the bottleneck that everything flowed through, I became the coach who helped others make good decisions." Maya smiled. "The team's capacity tripled within three months."

Takahashi's eyes widened. "Three times the throughput?"

"With better quality outcomes, because decisions were made closer to the actual work." Maya leaned forward. "But the most important metric was this: when I took a two-week vacation, security work continued smoothly. Nothing stalled waiting for me."

She could see the wheels turning in Takahashi's mind as he processed the implications.

"Your value isn't in making every decision," Maya said gently. "It's in building a system where good decisions happen naturally, with or without you."

Takahashi studied the diagrams, then looked up with newfound clarity. "I've been measuring the wrong things. Tracking how many reviews I complete instead of how many my team can handle independently."

"Exactly. You've optimized for your involvement rather than team capability." Maya drew a final diagram showing how decision authority could gradually shift. "This isn't about abdicating responsibility, it's about elevating your impact."

As understanding dawned in Takahashi's eyes, Maya felt that familiar satisfaction, the moment when a leader began to see beyond the immediate tactical pressures to the strategic opportunity. He wasn't just learning to delegate; he was discovering how to build lasting capability.

"Where do we start?" he asked, straightening his shoulders with fresh determination.

"By mapping your current workflow, identifying where you're the constraint, and creating decision frameworks that enable others to move forward safely." Maya smiled. "And by accepting that your greatest contribution might be stepping back from some decisions so you can focus on the ones that truly need your expertise."

Takahashi nodded, a new energy in his posture. "Building capability, not dependency."

"Exactly," Maya said. "That's how you create a legacy that outlasts your tenure."

* * *

"Don't worry," Maya said, noting the slight furrow in Takahashi's brow. "This isn't your failing. It's actually the most common trap for effective security leaders."

She leaned back in her chair, remembering a colleague who'd faced the same challenge.

"I worked with a CISO named Elaine at a healthcare company. Brilliant technical mind, she could solve any security problem put in front of her." Maya traced the edge of the diagram with her finger. "The board loved her because she always had answers. Her team respected her expertise. But when she looked at her calendar, it was wall-to-wall meetings, each one waiting for her decision."

Takahashi nodded in recognition.

"One day, Elaine had this realization that being the answer person was actually making her organization weaker, not stronger." Maya's voice softened with the memory. "So, she made a radical shift. When people came with questions, she stopped giving answers."

"What did she do instead?" Takahashi asked.

"She'd ask, 'What do you think we should do?' Then she'd guide them through their own analysis." Maya smiled. "At first, her team was frustrated. They just wanted the answer. But gradually, something changed. They started developing their own problem-solving muscles."

Maya drew a small diagram showing how capability spread across Elaine's organization.

"Within six months, her senior architects were handling complex security architecture decisions independently. Her managers were resolving conflicts without escalation. The organization developed a deeper security bench." Maya tapped the paper. "And Elaine? She finally had time to focus on strategic initiatives instead of tactical decisions."

Takahashi studied the diagram. "She became a teacher, not just a decision-maker."

"Exactly. She shifted from providing answers to building problem-solving capabilities." Maya gestured between them with a slight smile. "Not unlike what I'm doing right now."

They both paused, recognizing the meta-moment.

"I see what you did there," Takahashi said with a genuine laugh.

"The best teaching happens when you don't realize you're being taught," Maya replied. "Elaine's greatest achievement wasn't any specific security control she implemented. It was building an organization that could function effectively without her constant input."

She met Takahashi's gaze directly. "That's the difference between being important and being truly influential. Importance is when things can't happen without you. Influence is when things continue happening because of you, even in your absence."

* * *

The traditional izakaya buzzed with after-hours energy as servers brought another round of sake to the private room. Maya watched with amusement as Takahashi's team loosened their ties and shed the formality that had defined their earlier meetings. Three hours ago, they'd been discussing zero trust architecture; now they were debating song selections for the karaoke machine in the corner.

"Tran-san, you must sing next," insisted Hideo, the youngest security analyst on Takahashi's team. His cheeks flushed from both excitement and sake.

Maya laughed, raising her hands in mock surrender. "I promise my cybersecurity skills far exceed my singing abilities."

Takahashi smiled, more relaxed than Maya had seen him all week. "Even in karaoke, you Americans think of individual performance. For us, it's about the group harmony."

"That's actually a perfect metaphor for what we were discussing earlier," Maya said, accepting a small cup of sake. "Security leadership isn't about solo performances. It's about orchestrating something that continues playing beautifully, even when you step away from the conductor's stand."

Takahashi nodded appreciatively. "You never stop teaching, do you?"

"Occupational hazard," Maya admitted with a smile.

Her phone vibrated on the table. Maya glanced down to see Priya's name on the screen alongside a photo of server logs and a brief message: Caught this before it escalated. Your "capability not dependency" mantra paid off again. Drinks when you're back?

Maya's expression softened as she turned her phone to show Takahashi. "Speaking of building capability, this is from my former colleague, Priya Desai."

"The one who now runs security at FinEdge?" Takahashi asked, recognizing the name.

"The very same." Maya set her sake cup down. "When Priya first joined my team, she was technically brilliant but operationally isolated. Classic 'if you want something done right, do it yourself' mindset."

The table quieted as the team leaned in, sensing another valuable lesson embedded in the story.

"Priya would handle incidents alone, working through the night rather than waking teammates. She'd write detection rules but keep them in her personal repository." Maya smiled at the memory. "She was creating a dangerous dependency on herself, though she saw it as dedication."

"How did you change this?" asked Miyu, Takahashi's deputy CISO.

"I started by telling her I was going on vacation for two weeks, with no connectivity." Maya laughed. "You should have seen her face. Pure panic."

"That seems risky," Takahashi observed.

"It was calculated. Before leaving, I worked with her to document her processes, cross-train teammates, and create escalation paths." Maya's voice softened. "The key was helping her understand that her true value wasn't in being irreplaceable, but in building systems that reflected her expertise."

Maya glanced at the text message again. "When I returned, something had shifted. She'd discovered that her team could handle more than she expected, and that teaching others actually expanded her own influence."

"And now she leads security for a major financial technology company," Takahashi finished.

"Exactly. The leadership echo," Maya said. "By building capability in Priya rather than dependency, her growth became my legacy. Now she's doing the same with her team."

Maya raised her cup in a small toast. "The strongest security organizations aren't built around individual heroes. They're built by leaders who make heroics unnecessary."

The karaoke machine chimed, signaling its readiness. Maya smiled and gestured toward it.

"Now, shall we demonstrate how capability building works in karaoke? I suggest we all help improve each other's performances, though in my case, you'll need to build capability from scratch."

The room erupted in laughter as Takahashi's team eagerly began selecting songs, the security lesson seamlessly woven into their evening celebration.

* * *

The morning sun pierced through the hotel curtains with ruthless efficiency. Maya winced, reaching for the glass of water she'd wisely placed on her nightstand. Sake hangovers were their own special category of regret.

How did Takahashi's team do this? Last night they'd been singing until nearly midnight, and now they'd be bright-eyed for their 9 AM session. The Japanese work ethic was no myth, apparently.

After a quick shower and double espresso, Maya felt almost human again. She gathered her materials and headed to Takahashi's office, where his security team had already assembled in the conference room. True to her prediction, they looked frustratingly alert.

"Good morning, Tran-san," Takahashi greeted with a knowing smile. "I hope you slept well."

"Wonderfully," Maya lied, returning his smile. "Ready for our final day together."

As Maya set up her presentation on capability building, she noticed Ren, a junior analyst who'd been quiet during yesterday's sessions. He kept glancing at a small notebook, then back at her.

Midway through her presentation on security mentorship models, Maya paused. "Questions so far?"

Ren shifted in his seat, then raised his hand tentatively. Takahashi nodded encouragingly.

"Tran-san," Ren began, his voice gaining confidence, "you've shared many stories about developing others. Could you provide more practical methods? Specific techniques we could implement immediately?"

Maya set down her clicker, genuinely delighted by the question. "Absolutely, Ren. That's exactly what we should focus on."

She moved to the whiteboard. "First, look for teaching moments in daily work. When someone brings you a problem, resist solving it outright. Ask guiding questions instead: 'What have you tried?' 'Where might we look next?' This builds problem-solving muscles."

Maya drew a simple diagram showing skill progression. "Second, practice meaningful delegation. Not just assigning tasks, but transferring responsibility with context. Explain why a task matters, not just what needs doing."

She continued, energized by Ren's engagement. "Third, create scaffolded challenges, problems slightly beyond current abilities, but with support available. I keep a 'stretch assignment' inventory specifically for development opportunities."

"And finally," Maya concluded, "make reflection routine. After incidents or projects, hold brief retrospectives focused on growth rather than blame. Ask: 'What did we learn? How would we approach this differently next time?'"

Ren nodded, furiously taking notes.

"The most powerful capability builder," Maya added, "is simply believing people can grow beyond their current limitations. Your expectations shape their performance."

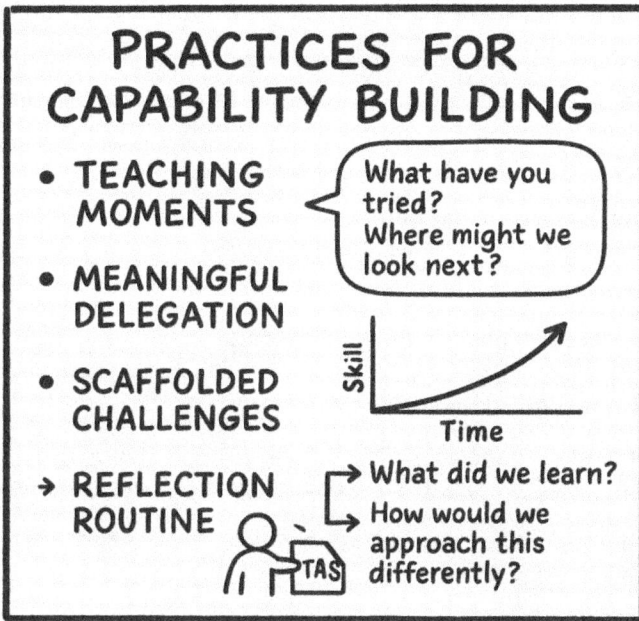

PRACTICES FOR CAPABILITY BUILDING

- TEACHING MOMENTS — *What have you tried? Where might we look next?*

- MEANINGFUL DELEGATION

- SCAFFOLDED CHALLENGES — *Skill / Time (graph)*

→ REFLECTION ROUTINE — *What did we learn? How would we approach this differently?*

* * *

Maya noticed the afternoon light shifting through the windows as they approached the end of their session. The energy in the room had transformed over these three days, from polite attention to genuine engagement. Even the most reserved team members were now contributing ideas.

"Before we wrap up," Maya said, "I'd like to try something different." She smiled, thinking of Callahan. The Gray Hat would often end their sessions by stepping back, creating space for others to articulate their own insights.

Time to pull a Callahan.

Maya moved to the side of the room. "Takahashi-san, would you and your team mind helping me explain something crucial? I'm curious about your perspective on what we might call 'the legacy effect.'"

Takahashi raised an eyebrow, intrigued by the shift.

"Security leadership isn't just about what we accomplish today," Maya continued. "It's about what continues after we're gone. I'd like to hear your thoughts on how we measure that kind of impact."

She gestured toward the whiteboard, then took a seat among the team members rather than standing at the front. The subtle repositioning instantly changed the dynamic.

After a moment's hesitation, Takahashi rose and approached the board. "Perhaps the true measure is not in the problems we solve," he said thoughtfully, "but in the problem-solvers we create."

Ren, emboldened by the earlier exchange, added, "Documentation and processes matter, but people who understand the 'why' behind them matter more."

Maya nodded, watching the team build on each other's insights. This was exactly what she'd hoped for – not just absorbing concepts but internalizing and expressing them in their own words.

As their session concluded, Takahashi walked Maya to the elevator. "A clever technique, Tran-san. Having us articulate the lessons ourselves."

Maya smiled. "The best ideas are the ones people discover for themselves. Or at least believe they did."

"Ah," Takahashi said with knowing appreciation. "Building capability, not dependency – even in how you teach about building capability."

"Exactly," Maya replied. "The ultimate legacy isn't what people remember you saying, but what they find themselves thinking long after you're gone."

* * *

Maya slid the keycard into her hotel room door, that familiar electronic chirp greeting her for what felt like the thousandth time. Different hotel, same routine. She kicked off her shoes and collapsed onto the bed, staring at the ceiling.

The session with Takahashi's team had gone exceptionally well. They'd transformed from passive recipients to active participants, taking ownership of the security concepts she'd shared. It was exactly the outcome she'd hoped for.

So why did this success feel hollow?

Maya pulled out her laptop, scanning through her calendar. Tokyo today, Singapore next week, then New York, Chicago, and back to San Francisco. The cities blurred together in her mind – a never-ending carousel of airports, hotels, and conference rooms.

Her phone buzzed. A text from Callahan: "You're headed home."

Maya frowned. Was this some cryptic acknowledgment of her travel schedule? She hadn't mentioned her itinerary to him. She was about to respond when another message appeared.

"Not to your apartment. Home. Where you belong."

She sat up, puzzling over his meaning. Before she could reply, her phone rang. Callahan.

"I sensed a disturbance in the force," he said without preamble.

Maya laughed despite herself. "You have an uncanny timing."

"You're building capability in others, Maya. That's good. But it's not the end."

"What do you mean?" She walked to the window, looking out at Tokyo's glittering skyline.

"It's the beginning of greater impact." His voice had that familiar Zen-master quality. "You're teaching people to fish. Excellent. But what if you could design better fishing rods? Or transform the entire fishing industry?"

Maya was quiet, letting his words sink in.

"You've mastered the art of building security capability in organizations," Callahan continued. "But you're still just visiting. What if you stopped being the wandering guru and started building something permanent?"

The question hit her like a physical force. Building something. Creating, not just advising.

"The question isn't whether you're good at what you do," Callahan said softly. "The question is whether what you're doing is your highest contribution."

Maya watched the city lights, feeling something shift inside her. "What comes next?" she whispered.

"That's for you to decide," Callahan replied. "But I suspect it involves putting down roots somewhere. Creating something that outlasts a three-day workshop."

After they hung up, Maya remained at the window, her mind racing with possibilities that suddenly seemed both terrifying and exhilarating.

Chapter 15:

The Security Influencer's Path Forward

Maya never thought of starting a business. She didn't consider herself an entrepreneur. Yet here she was, three months after that night in Tokyo, sitting on a park bench with a rapidly melting blue raspberry snow cone, watching teenagers perfect kickflips and ollies at the skate park.

The duck pond beside her rippled with afternoon light. She'd walked this park countless times as a security consultant, always passing through, never fully present. Now she found herself noticing details – how the ducks formed temporary alliances, how the skaters had an unspoken code about taking turns, how the security guard at the far entrance checked the same spots at the same intervals.

Systems within systems. Patterns everywhere.

"Most people look at that pond and see ducks," Callahan said, appearing beside her as if he'd been there all along. Today, he wore khakis and a faded DEF CON shirt under his blazer. "You see territorial negotiations and resource allocation strategies."

Maya smiled. "Hazard of the profession."

"Or its gift." Callahan produced his own snow cone – bright pink – from seemingly nowhere. "How's unemployment treating you?"

"I prefer 'strategic sabbatical,'" Maya corrected, watching a teenage girl land a complex trick to appreciative nods from older skaters. "Though Elena keeps texting me about joining her startup."

"Ah, the siren call of someone else's vision." Callahan's eyes crinkled. "Safer than building your own."

Maya turned to study him. "You've been pushing me toward something specific all along, haven't you?"

"I merely illuminate paths. You choose which to walk." He took a bite of his snow cone. "Though I admit, watching you outgrow every container has been satisfying."

A duck waddled near their bench, eyeing them hopefully.

"Security concepts are as old as human history," Callahan continued, gesturing toward the pond. "Territory. Trust. Verification. But their application evolves constantly."

Maya nodded. "Like those skaters. The fundamental physics haven't changed, but what they can do with a board keeps expanding."

"Precisely." Callahan leaned forward. "You've mastered teaching others to navigate today's threats. But what about tomorrow's? What about creating the frameworks that will outlast specific technologies?"

Maya felt that familiar tug – the pull toward creation rather than reaction. "I've been sketching something. A methodology for organizations to develop security intuition, not just compliance."

"Tell me more." Callahan's attention was complete, present.

As Maya outlined her nascent idea – a blend of organizational psychology, threat modeling, and strategic communication – she felt energy building. This wasn't just another consulting framework. This was something new.

"The world doesn't need another security consultant," she finished. "It needs new ways to think about security itself."

Callahan nodded slowly. "And there it is."

"There what is?"

"Your next evolution." He stood, brushing invisible dust from his pants. "Influence isn't a destination, Maya. It's a continuous journey. The moment you think you've mastered it is precisely when you become irrelevant."

Maya watched a new group of skaters arrive, studying the established crew before joining in. "Like security itself."

"Like life." Callahan dropped his snow cone stick in a nearby trash can. "The question isn't whether you'll start something new. It's whether you'll have the courage to let it become something you can't fully control."

He walked away without a goodbye, leaving Maya with half-melted blue syrup and a mind full of possibilities. She pulled out her notebook – not to capture someone else's wisdom this time, but to sketch the outline of her own.

Maya stood center stage, a single spotlight highlighting her against the massive conference hall's darkness. The RSAC logo glowed on screens throughout the venue, casting blue light across thousands of faces. Three thousand security professionals stared back at her, CISOs, analysts, engineers, and vendors, all waiting for her next words.

Strange how the perspective shifted from up here. She'd sat in those same seats for over a decade, notebook in hand, always the student. Always learning. Always thinking others had more wisdom to share than she did.

The weight of the presentation clicker felt unfamiliar in her palm. Maya glanced down at her simple black blazer and remembered how she'd agonized over what to wear. Not too corporate. Not too casual. Something that said "I belong here, but I'm not trying too hard to prove it."

Behind her, the slide displayed an elegant visualization of interconnected nodes forming a neural network pattern. The words "Adaptive Influence: Security Leadership in Changing Landscapes" floated above it.

She took a breath. The silence had stretched just long enough to be noticeable.

"Security is fundamentally a human discipline," Maya said, her voice carrying through the sound system with a confidence that surprised even her. "Our technologies change. Our threats evolve. But the core of what we do, building trust and influencing behavior, remains constant."

She clicked to the next slide, revealing a timeline of security paradigms.

"I've spent fifteen years watching our industry chase solutions. Firewalls. Then, endpoint protection. The,n zero trust. Each technological wave promises to solve our problems." Maya paused, scanning the audience. "But the breaches keep happening. Not because our technologies fail, but because our influence fails."

Outside the conference hall windows, San Francisco spring sunshine bathed the city. Inside, attendees shifted in their seats, some nodding, others typing notes.

"Two booths down from here, there's an F1 racing car," Maya continued, earning scattered laughter. "Beautiful engineering. Completely irrelevant to what that company actually does. But it gets your attention."

More laughter, louder this time.

"I'm not here to criticize their marketing choices. I'm actually envious. They understand something fundamental that many security leaders miss: attention precedes influence."

She clicked again, revealing a framework diagram.

"The methods I'm sharing today aren't revolutionary. They're evolutionary. They're what I've learned by failing, repeatedly and sometimes spectacularly, to move security forward in organizations that viewed it as an obstacle rather than an enabler."

Maya caught sight of Callahan in the back row, arms crossed, that knowing half-smile on his face. She hadn't invited him. Somehow, he always appeared at inflection points in her journey.

"The core principles of influence haven't changed since Aristotle identified ethos, pathos, and logos. What changes is how we apply them in contexts of increasing complexity and speed."

As she walked the audience through her framework, Maya felt a strange doubling of perspective, seeing herself from outside, standing where she'd always believed others belonged. How many insights had she swallowed over the years, thinking they weren't valuable enough to share?

"Security challenges will continue to evolve," she said, approaching her conclusion. "Our technological responses must adapt. But our human approach to influence, building trust, speaking in others' languages, creating ownership, these are timeless."

She clicked to her final slide: a simple question mark.

"Our responsibility isn't just to apply these principles, but to evolve them. To teach them. To ensure the next generation of security leaders doesn't have to learn them through the same painful trial and error that many of us did."

Maya smiled, the spotlight warm on her face.

"That's our legacy. Not the controls we implement, but the capability we build in others to carry this work forward."

* * *

The applause washed over Maya as she stepped away from the podium. Hands reached out to shake hers as she navigated the crowd. Questions, business cards, and LinkedIn connection requests followed her as she made her way to the book signing area.

Her face stared back at her from a stack of hardcovers on the table. The Security Influencer: Building Trust in a Zero-Trust World. Maya Ellison Tran, author. The silver embossed letters caught the convention center lighting, making her name shimmer slightly. How did this happen? When did this happen? Maya knew the answer, eighteen months of early mornings, late nights, and countless revisions, but it didn't feel real sometimes.

Who knew she had enough information to put down in a book and write it in a way that others would pick up and read it? Yet here they were, forming a line that snaked through the exhibition hall.

The convention organizer handed her a pen. "Ready, Ms. Tran?"

Maya nodded, taking her seat behind the table. "Thank you for arranging this."

"Are you kidding? We're thrilled. Your session was one of the first to sell out."

She needed this information to spread further than one consulting engagement at a time. Security professionals were adapting to new business models and technology landscapes. So must the leaders sharing their knowledge with peers and following generations.

A young woman with bright eyes and a determined expression approached the table first, clutching the book to her chest.

"Ms. Tran, I can't believe I'm meeting you in person." She placed the book on the table with reverent care. "I'm Zoe. I just started as a SOC analyst three months ago, and your gh05t5c1pt blogs have been really helpful in getting perspective."

Maya felt her cheeks warm. "You follow my blog?"

"Follow it? I have notifications turned on for your new posts." Zoe laughed nervously. "Is that weird? That's probably weird."

"Not weird. Flattering." Maya opened the book. "Who should I make this out to?"

"Zoe Phillips. And if you could just... I don't know, any advice for someone just starting out?"

Maya thought for a moment, then began writing. When she finished, she handed the book back with a smile.

After Maya signed the book and wrote a beautiful note to the wonderful young woman who introduced herself as a new SOC analyst, she looked up to see a man with a gray blazer over a t-shirt, a unicorn hat perched ridiculously on his head.

"You're kidding me," she said, unable to suppress a grin.

Callahan approached the table, casual as ever despite the absurd hat. "The mighty gh05t5c1pt, signing books like a proper celebrity."

"You're embarrassing me."

"Good. Keeps you humble." He slid a copy of her book across the table. "I'll take your autograph too, if you don't mind."

Maya rolled her eyes but opened the book. "Where would you like it?"

Goofy guy opened the book to his signature at the end of the foreword he wrote for this book. Weirdo.

"Right next to mine," he said, tapping the page. "Seems fitting."

Maya glanced at his words, the foreword she'd read a dozen times during editing, but still made her emotional. His belief in her work had made this possible.

"To Callahan," she wrote, "who taught me that influence isn't about having all the answers, but asking better questions. Thank you for showing up when I needed guidance most."

She handed the book back. "Happy?"

"Ecstatic." He tucked the book under his arm. "Your talk was excellent, by the way."

"You actually sat through the whole thing?"

"Front to back. I even took notes." He produced his weathered Moleskine. "Old habits."

Maya shook her head. "You never change."

"Neither do you," Callahan said with a wink. "And that's why this, " he gestured to the line of people waiting, "is just the beginning."

* * *

Six months later, Maya adjusted her headphones as Perry Whitaker's voice came through crystal clear in her home office.

"Welcome back to Security Career Compass. I'm Perry Whitaker, and today I'm joined by Maya Ellison Tran, CISO, consultant, and author of the bestselling 'The Security Influencer.' Maya, thanks for making time for us."

"Thanks for having me, Perry. Love what you're doing for the community."

Perry's enthusiastic voice filled her ears. "So today's big question, one my listeners have been flooding my inbox about since announcing you'd be on, what is the top thing both new and experienced cyber professionals need to know?"

Maya smiled, gazing at the framed photo on her desk, her first security team from years ago. "It's about becoming a transformational leader, regardless of your title. I've watched countless brilliant technical people hit glass ceilings they built themselves."

"Can you unpack that a bit?"

"When I started as a security architect, I thought technical excellence was everything. I built beautiful security designs." Maya laughed. "That nobody implemented. It wasn't until I started asking different questions that things changed."

"What kind of questions?"

"Instead of 'how do we secure this?' I started asking, 'How do we help this business initiative succeed safely?' The shift seems subtle, but it's revolutionary."

Maya traced the journey from her early days to her CISO role. "As a CISO, I realized my job wasn't cybersecurity, it was business transformation through the lens of security. When I focused on enabling business outcomes rather than preventing bad security practices, everything changed. Suddenly, I wasn't fighting for budget; I was partnering on innovation."

"That's powerful," Perry said. "Any specific examples you can share?"

"There was this product launch where marketing needed to collect customer data. Traditional security would say 'no' or add friction. Instead, we partnered to design a process that was both secure and improved conversion rates. The CMO became my biggest ally after that."

Maya leaned forward. "As a consultant now, I see the pattern everywhere. The security leaders who transform their organizations don't just know security, they understand business language, they build relationships before crises, and they make security part of the value proposition."

"So it's not about the technical skills?"

"Technical skills get you in the door. Transformation skills get you a seat at the table. And ultimately, that's where security has its greatest impact, not in preventing bad things, but in enabling great things to happen safely."

* * *

Maya stepped into the converted warehouse space in Brussels, its industrial beams now adorned with soft lighting and interactive digital displays. The annual European Security Leadership Summit had transformed from the stiff, technical conference she'd first attended years ago into something more dynamic, more human.

"Maya! Everything's set for your workshop in Hall C," called out Elise, the event coordinator, tablet in hand. "We've got breakout tables arranged in pods like you requested, and the interactive boards are synced to your presentation."

"Perfect, thanks." Maya scanned the space, taking in the scene with quiet satisfaction. Last year, she'd been just another attendee. Now, she was leading the summit's flagship workshop: "The Ripple Effect: How Security Approaches Transform Organizational Functions."

She checked her watch, still forty minutes before her session. Time enough to walk the floor and gauge the energy. As she moved through the main exhibition hall, she spotted familiar faces leading discussions at various tables. Johan from Amsterdam's financial sector, Martine from the French privacy commission, and even Carlos from her old consulting days, all colleagues who'd become friends over years of shared struggles and victories.

Near the refreshment area, Maya paused at the edge of a small group session. A woman she didn't recognize was gesturing enthusiastically.

"So the CISO tells the CFO, 'I'm not asking for budget to prevent something bad. I'm investing in making our customer experience more trustworthy than our competitors.' And just like that, funding approved!"

The group laughed appreciatively.

Maya tilted her head, brow furrowing. That story sounded familiar; it was about her conversation with a particularly difficult CFO at TechForward three years ago. But she hadn't written about it in her book, and she was certain she hadn't shared it at any conferences.

She approached after the group dispersed. "That was a great anecdote about the CISO and CFO."

The woman turned, surprised. Her eyes widened with recognition. "Oh! You're Maya Tran! I'm Sophie. I work for Priya Desai now."

"Small world," Maya smiled. "That story you told, about the CISO reframing security as customer trust?"

"Yes! Priya uses it all the time when she's coaching us on executive communications. Wait, " Sophie's expression shifted to embarrassment. "That was about you, wasn't it?"

Maya nodded, a warm feeling spreading through her chest. "Priya never mentioned she still tells that story."

"Are you kidding? She has a whole repertoire of 'Maya methods,' as she calls them. She made us read your book, but the stories she tells from when you worked together, those are what really stick."

As Maya walked toward her workshop hall, she felt a peculiar mix of humility and pride. Her ideas weren't just spreading through her own words, but through the words of others who had taken them, applied them, and passed them on, sometimes without even knowing their origin.

In Hall C, attendees were already filtering in, arranging themselves at tables. Maya noticed Priya across the room, directing her team to different discussion groups. Their eyes met, and Priya gave a small, knowing nod before turning back to her conversation.

Maya activated her presentation display, watching as the title illuminated the screens around the room: "The Ripple Effect." She hadn't fully appreciated the truth of that title until now. Security influence wasn't just about what you personally accomplished; it was about how your approaches continued to spread long after you'd moved on, carried forward by others who found value in them.

As she stepped to the center of the room to begin, Maya realized: this was the true measure of transformation. Not what you changed directly, but what changes you inspired others to create.

* * *

Maya stirred her mediocre convention center coffee, leaning back in the uncomfortable plastic chair. DEF CON's cafeteria buzzed with the peculiar energy that only happens when thousands of hackers, security professionals, and curious outsiders converge in one place. No other conference quite matched its chaotic authenticity.

She'd come with minimal expectations this year. No keynote, no major presentation, just a friend's request to help launch the new Architecture Village and run a workshop on security architecture fundamentals. After years of advocating that security architecture deserved its own space alongside the red team and blue team villages, she felt a quiet satisfaction seeing it finally materialize.

Maya sipped her coffee and let the conversations around her filter in. At the next table, three twenty-somethings with multi-colored hair and laptop stickers from obscure CTF competitions were debating the merits of different cloud security posture management tools. Behind her, someone was explaining zero-knowledge proofs to an increasingly confused listener.

A particularly animated group caught her attention, consisting of four people, probably mid-career professionals based on their conversation, speaking just loud enough that eavesdropping required minimal effort.

"I just attended that talk about continuous development," said a woman with thick-rimmed glasses. "I wouldn't say it was ground-shattering, but it is incredibly important. Amazingly, it wasn't just about technical skills or communication. This one was about continuing to grow your influence and impact. It reminded me of Wade's cult presentation and the pyramid of pain."

Maya suppressed a smile. She'd given that talk yesterday in one of the smaller tracks. The title had been deliberately understated: "Security Career Longevity: Beyond Burnout and Plateaus." No mention of her name or credentials in the program, just the content. That was the beauty of DEF CON. Nobody cared who you were, just what you knew and were willing to share.

"I liked how she talked about measuring impact beyond your immediate team," added another person at their table. "The ripple effect concept really stuck with me."

Maya felt a small wave of satisfaction. Not pride, she'd learned to let go of that years ago, but the simple contentment of knowing her ideas had resonated with someone. She hadn't even introduced herself at the beginning of the talk. This crowd didn't care about accolades, degrees, or certifications. They just wanted to know cool stuff and hack all the things, even careers and life.

She gazed across the crowded cafeteria, reflecting on her own journey. From anxious security analyst to confident CISO, from technical specialist to strategic leader, from seeking validation to giving others a platform. Each step had seemed so consequential in the moment, yet now formed just one thread in a much larger tapestry.

"Hey, boss! Have you heard of this Angelina Jolie movie, Hackers? It's like super old. They're playing it in the theater tonight. I heard they had to find something called a VCR to play it."

Jessica Huang's voice snapped Maya from her reverie. The security intern stood there, holding a tray loaded with convention center pizza and an energy drink, her DEF CON badge dangling with far too many ribbons attached.

Maya laughed. "Yes, I've heard of it. And no, they won't be using a VCR. Though I'm old enough to have owned several."

"You want to go? I've heard it's hilariously bad, but also kind of amazing. A bunch of us from the Architecture Village are meeting up there."

Maya considered the invitation. Ten years ago, she'd have skipped it to prepare for tomorrow's workshop. Five years ago, she'd have gone but spent the whole time networking. Now?

"Sounds perfect," she said, gathering her things. "Just promise not to laugh too hard when I tell you I had that exact same haircut as Angelina in the mid-90s."

* * *

Maya walked beside Jessica toward the theater, feeling a wave of nostalgia wash over her. The young woman's enthusiasm reminded Maya of herself at that age, eager, absorbing everything, not yet realizing how much she already knew.

"So what's the secret?" Jessica asked suddenly, adjusting her oversized DEF CON hoodie. "To all of this. To becoming... well, you."

Maya laughed. "There's no secret formula, Jessica."

"Come on. There has to be something. You've built this amazing career. People actually listen when you speak. They implement your ideas." Jessica's eyes were earnest behind her glasses. "What made the difference?"

Maya considered the question as they navigated through the crowded hallway. What had been the key to her success? What principles had truly mattered?

"If I had to distill it," Maya said finally, "it would come down to a few core principles that connect everything else."

She paused as they reached the theater entrance, where a group of twenty-somethings were already gathered, debating the technical inaccuracies they expected to mock during the screening.

"First, speak their language, not your expertise," Maya explained. "I spent years thinking technical brilliance would win arguments. But I learned that clarity matters more than complexity. Translating security concepts into language others understand, that's what gets action."

Jessica nodded, taking mental notes.

"Second, lead with empathy, not alerts. Understanding what matters to others gives you the influence to actually protect them. When you recognize their constraints and priorities, you can align security with what they already value."

"That makes sense," Jessica said. "What else?"

"Frame security in terms of business outcomes," Maya continued. "Security for security's sake is a hard sell. But security that enables revenue, protects reputation, or accelerates time-to-market? That gets funded."

Maya ticked off the principles on her fingers as they found seats in the back row.

"Build trust through consistency, not control. Make security their idea, not your mandate. Collaborate on solutions, don't dictate requirements. Build coalitions before you need them."

Jessica's eyes widened. "That's a lot to remember."

"They're all connected," Maya explained. "Each principle builds on the others. When you speak others' language and lead with empathy, you can frame security in business terms. That builds trust, which helps you create ownership and collaboration, which strengthens your coalitions."

"And the operational stuff?" Jessica pressed. "The flow management and friction reduction you talked about yesterday?"

Maya smiled. "Those are equally important. Manage workflow, not just work volume. Make secure behavior the path of least resistance. Build a security culture, not just awareness."

She leaned back in her seat as the lights dimmed. "And finally, lead through clarity, not authority, and build a legacy of capability, not dependency."

Jessica absorbed this in silence as the movie's opening credits began to roll.

"So that's it?" she whispered. "The complete Maya Tran playbook for security influence?"

Maya shook her head, smiling in the darkness. "The principles stay the same, but how you apply them evolves constantly. The security landscape changes. Business models transform. Technologies advance. But influence, true, lasting influence, always comes back to these fundamentals."

"Building bridges between security and what matters to others," Jessica summarized.

"Exactly," Maya said softly. "Technical skills get you in the door. But these principles? They're what make security actually happen."

As the infamous "HACK THE PLANET!" scene played out on screen to cheers from the audience, Maya felt a deep sense of contentment. The principles she'd discovered, refined, and shared over her career weren't just techniques; they were a philosophy for making security matter in a world that often saw it as an obstacle.

And watching Jessica's thoughtful expression in the flickering light, Maya knew the influence would continue long after her own career ended. The ripple effect had only just begun.

* * *

After the movie ended, Maya lingered in the theater as others filed out. Jessica had rushed off to another session, energized with new ideas and connections to explore. Maya found a quiet corner in the now-empty room and pulled out her journal, a habit she'd maintained for years, capturing insights that might otherwise slip away.

She smiled, thinking about the countless security professionals who, like Jessica, were trying to navigate this complex landscape. The technical skills were crucial, but insufficient on their own. The real challenge was making security matter to people who didn't speak its language.

Hello, reader, she wrote, as if addressing an invisible audience. You made it through. You've read the principles, absorbed the examples, and perhaps recognized parts of your own journey along the way. But the real question isn't what you've read, it's what you'll do with it.

Maya paused, tapping her pen against the page.

These concepts and examples aren't just theoretical exercises; they're invitations to transform how you approach security leadership. They're tools to help you become a trusted advisor to your business, not just its guardian.

She glanced up at the blank screen where, minutes earlier, characters had dramatized an outdated vision of what hacking and security meant. The real work was far less cinematic but infinitely more impactful.

There's so much to know in cybersecurity, and no two journeys look exactly alike. Not everyone will become a CISO, and honestly, not everyone wants to. Personally, there isn't enough money in the world to convince me to take that particular role.

Maya smiled at her own candor.

Whatever your position in this field, I hope these principles help you evolve from a guardian to a guide. The difference is subtle but profound. A guardian stands apart, protecting from the outside. A guide walks alongside, illuminating the path forward.

The goal isn't just to connect with the business, it's to become truly part of it. When security speaks the language of business outcomes, when it empowers rather than obstructs, it transforms from a necessary cost into a strategic advantage.

The principles in these pages aren't the end of your journey. They're the beginning of your impact.

The Security Influence Playbook

Security doesn't end when the dashboard lights turn green. It doesn't begin with a policy or finish with an audit. And it certainly doesn't live exclusively in the SOC or on the CISO's desk.

The truth is, security lives or dies in the daily decisions people make across your organization. Decisions about timelines, features, vendors, shortcuts, budgets, architecture, and trust. Every one of those decisions is shaped by influence. Not authority. Not alerts. Influence.

And influence, unlike access control, can't be granted. It has to be earned.

This book has walked you through Maya's journey, from technical leader to strategic partner. You've seen how translation changes outcomes, how empathy unlocks visibility, and how reframing risk in business terms opens doors that technical accuracy alone cannot.

But if you've ever finished a story like this and wondered, "Okay, but what do I actually do next?", this chapter is for you.

What follows isn't a checklist. It's not another framework or maturity model. It's a playbook: a collection of operating principles for security professionals who want to be more than correct; they want to be effective.

Each principle in this chapter is drawn directly from the real-world examples you've read: reframed conversations, high-stakes decisions, moments where influence turned the tide. These are not abstract ideals; they're practical disciplines. They've been tested in boardrooms, on engineering floors, and during 3 a.m. incidents where clarity was scarce and stakes were high.

This playbook is organized functionally. Because in the real world, you don't act based on chapters, you act based on context:

Each principle includes a clear description, the reason it matters, and how to apply it tomorrow, not theoretically, but practically. And at the end of the chapter, you'll find a one-page quick reference, just enough to scan in the hallway on your way to a high-stakes meeting.

Use this chapter however you need to:

Approach it like Maya would: not as gospel, but as guidance. Adjust it to suit your style, context, and culture. But hold to the core idea: Security isn't a function you enforce. It's a capability you enable. And influence is the lever that makes that possible.

Let's begin.

* * *

Part I: Communication

How you talk about security determines whether anyone listens.

Technical skill is not the barrier to influence in most organizations; language is. The way you communicate shapes how others perceive your priorities, your credibility, and your relevance. Speak only in security terms, and you'll get compliance at best and confusion at worst. But translate your message into the language of business, product, and operations, and you'll find traction where resistance used to live.

Here are the principles that will help you be heard, and more importantly, acted upon.

1. Translate, Don't Transmit

What it means: Stop assuming others will understand, or care about, your security expertise as-is. Your job is not to recite technical details. It's to interpret them into something others can value and act on.

Why it matters: Most security communication fails because it's a monologue of technical correctness. But people don't act on what they don't understand. Translation creates shared understanding and actionable clarity.

How to apply it tomorrow: Take one security issue you're tracking, just one, and rewrite it from your audience's perspective. If it's a dev team, connect it to performance, delivery timelines, or user experience. If it's the CFO, link it to cost, contract risk, or operational continuity. Speak their language, not yours. You'll see the difference immediately.

What it means: Lead with a narrative. Humans remember stories, not spreadsheets. Frame the risk, challenge, or proposal in a scenario that connects emotionally and practically, then support it with evidence.

Why it matters: Executives, engineers, and analysts all process stories more intuitively than data. Stories make risk real. They provide context for why something matters, not just that it exists.

How to apply it tomorrow: Next time you present a finding or recommendation, begin with a short scenario: "Imagine we're two weeks from launch and a customer discovers..." or "Last month, a competitor suffered a breach when..." Then follow with your analysis. This isn't about fearmongering, it's about making abstract risk concrete.

3. Speak Their Metrics, Not Your Acronyms

What it means: Executives don't care about CVSS scores, SIEM events, or OWASP top 10 lists. They care about metrics like churn, time-to-market, revenue, and cost. Frame security in terms that they already track.

Why it matters: Every role in the business has its own scoreboard. If you can show how security moves their numbers in the right direction, or prevents them from falling, you become an ally, not an outsider.

How to apply it tomorrow: Before any cross-functional meeting, write down one metric your audience cares about. Ask yourself: "How does this security issue influence that number?" Lead with that. For example: "This delay isn't about patching, it's about missing our compliance window and stalling a deal worth $3.2 million."

Part II: Relationship Building

Security isn't enforced. It's invited.

Influence doesn't come from your title, your technical depth, or the size of your budget. It comes from trust, and trust is built one relationship at a time. Security professionals who isolate themselves become easy to ignore. Those who invest in relationships earn the right to be heard before there's a crisis.

This section is about becoming someone your colleagues want to work with, not because they're afraid of you, but because they trust you'll make them better.

4. Lead with Curiosity

What it means: Start conversations with genuine interest in the other person's goals, constraints, and pressures. Ask before advising. Understand before recommending.

Why it matters: When people feel interrogated, they shut down. When they feel understood, they open up. Curiosity invites collaboration whereas criticism creates resistance.

How to apply it tomorrow: Replace "Why didn't you follow the policy?" with "What were you trying to achieve when you made that choice?" In sprint planning, ask, "Where do you see potential risks here?" Let them surface issues instead of waiting for you to point them out. You'll learn more and solve more by listening first.

5. Build Trust Before You Need It

What it means: Trust isn't earned during an incident. It's earned long before one. Establish credibility through consistency, follow-through, and a strong presence.

Why it matters: When everything is on fire, no one has time to vet your intentions. If people already trust you, they'll follow your lead. If they don't, you'll waste time proving yourself while the damage spreads.

How to apply it tomorrow: Start small. Show up to their meetings, not just yours. Offer help with a low-stakes problem. Follow up on what you say. If you promise a review by Friday, deliver it Thursday. Trust builds when your actions consistently match your words.

6. Make Security Their Idea

What it means: Invite others into the solution space. When people contribute to the outcome, they take ownershi of itp. When you impose, they resist, even if they agree with the solution.

Why it matters: Influence isn't about being right. It's about helping others arrive at the right conclusion in a way that makes them feel empowered, not overruled.

How to apply it tomorrow: Instead of saying, "We need to implement X," try: "What would it look like if we improved this control?" Or, "How could we make this safer without slowing you down?" Seed the idea, shape the direction, but let them carry it forward. You'll get commitment instead of compliance.

Part III: Decision Influence

Make security make sense where decisions happen.

Decisions aren't made in a vacuum. They happen in meetings, hallway conversations, spreadsheets, and emails. If you want security to be part of those decisions, you have to show up in a form that decision-makers can use. That means less technical defense, more strategic offense.

This section is about helping others choose the right thing, not because you insisted, but because you made it the obvious path.

7. Frame Risk in Business Terms

What it means: Translate technical risk into financial, reputational, legal, or operational impact. Use the language of outcomes, not the language of incidents.

Why it matters: "Unpatched system" doesn't resonate. "Delaying this patch could result in a $2.1 million SLA breach if we get hit this quarter" does. Executives don't need to know how the exploit works; they need to know what it could cost.

How to apply it tomorrow: Recast your next risk report with one column: "What could happen to the business?" Tie each item to a specific cost, delay, lost opportunity, or reputational hit. You'll stop getting blank stares and start getting decisions.

8. Offer Choices, Not Ultimatums

What it means: Present multiple paths to safety, not just the one you prefer. Let stakeholders choose their level of risk, within reason.

Why it matters: People resist being cornered. They respond better to agency. Giving options shows respect and makes them part of the decision-making process, which leads to better buy-in and fewer workarounds.

How to apply it tomorrow: Next time you recommend a fix, bring two options: "Here's the fastest fix with moderate risk," and "Here's the slower fix that's more robust." Explain the trade-offs clearly. Let them choose based on business priorities, not fear of your reaction.

9. Use Empathy as a Strategy, Not a Sentiment

What it means: Empathy isn't about being nice, it's about being smart. When you understand others' pressures, you can anticipate objections and shape your message accordingly.

Why it matters: Empathy gives you a predictive advantage. You can spot blockers before they show up. You can craft proposals that fit into their world instead of clashing with it.

How to apply it tomorrow: Before your next recommendation, write down what your audience is optimizing for. Is it speed? Budget? Customer trust? Then adjust your framing: "This control reduces your incident response time" is more persuasive to Ops than "It's required by policy."

Part IV: Team Culture & Leadership

The security culture you create is the one your team will replicate.

You can't influence the business if you don't lead your own team well. Influence starts inside. The way you respond to incidents, feedback, and failure becomes the model your team uses in every interaction they have. If you lead with fear, they'll pass on fear. If you lead with empathy and clarity, they'll pass on influence.

This section focuses on the internal habits that foster resilient, trusted, and effective security teams.

10. Replace Blame with Inquiry

What it means: Don't ask "Who did this?" Ask, "What made this the best choice at the time?" Treat mistakes as information, not indictments.

Why it matters: Fear kills visibility. If your team is afraid to speak up, you'll always be solving the wrong problem. Inquiry creates psychological safety, the foundation of a high-trust, high-performance team.

How to apply it tomorrow: During your next postmortem or code review, start with one question: "What made sense to you when you made that choice?" You'll surface constraints, assumptions, and breakdowns you never would've found with blame.

What it means: Make it safe to say, "I don't know," "I need help," or "I made a mistake." That's how you find real risk before it becomes a real incident.

Why it matters: People don't hide mistakes because they're malicious; they hide them because they're scared. Safety doesn't mean coddling. It means creating an environment where truth takes precedence over hierarchy.

How to apply it tomorrow: Share your own mistakes first. Normalize uncertainty. Say, "I missed that too," or "I used to think the same thing." It's not weakness, it's permission. And it makes your team stronger.

12. Design for Human Behavior, Not Ideal Policy

What it means: If your controls depend on perfect behavior, they will fail. Build systems that account for shortcuts, fatigue, and workarounds, not just intentions.

Why it matters: Security often breaks where people break. Ignoring human nature isn't a design choice; it's a blind spot. Good security doesn't punish reality. It anticipates it.

How to apply it tomorrow: Find one policy that's routinely bypassed and ask why. Then redesign it. Make the secure path the easy path. Better to have an imperfect control that's used than a perfect one that's ignored.

Part V: Operational Execution

The most effective security strategy is one that is actually implemented.

Great ideas don't matter if they never make it out of the slide deck. Security must work at the speed of business, not in opposition to it. Execution is where influence becomes tangible, where controls, conversations, and culture turn into outcomes.

This section is about embedding security in the daily rhythm of the organization so it becomes a habit, not overhead.

13. Align Security with Velocity

What it means: Security should be designed to accelerate delivery, not slow it down. Partner early, shape architecture, and reduce friction before it becomes failure.

Why it matters: When security lags behind, it becomes a blocker. When it runs alongside, it becomes an accelerator. The earlier you're involved, the more you can shape without obstructing your progress.

How to apply it tomorrow: Join your product or engineering teams' next sprint planning or design session. Ask, "What's coming that we can help de-risk now?" Get upstream, stay visible, and show that security doesn't just say "no", it asks, "how can we help?"

14. Build Security In, Don't Bolt It On

What it means: Retrofits are expensive, fragile, and unpopular. Security should be an integral part of the design, not an afterthought or a checklist.

Why it matters: When you integrate security early, it's cheaper, simpler, and more effective. When you tack it on later, it breaks things and breeds resentment.

How to apply it tomorrow: Pick one ongoing initiative, product launch, infrastructure migration, vendor onboarding, and embed a security presence early. Review the architecture, threat model the use case, or contribute to the design doc. Become part of "how we build," not just "how we review."

15. Communicate Security Readiness, Not Just Maturity

What it means: Don't focus only on how secure you look on paper. Focus on how prepared you are to detect, respond, and recover when, not if, things go wrong.

Why it matters: Maturity models reward structure. Attackers exploit blind spots. Executive stakeholders prioritize resilience over rigor.

How to apply it tomorrow: In your next board update or leadership report, show how fast your team identified a real incident or mitigated a risk, not just how many controls you've implemented. Demonstrate adaptability, not just audit readiness.

Security Kneeboard:
Quick Reference in Flight

You don't pull out a 300-page manual during an engine failure. You reach for the kneeboard.

This section isn't for training days or long-form reflection. It's for those high-pressure moments when you need a fast mental reset, a guiding phrase, a decision prompt. It's your in-flight reference, compact, field-ready distillation of the playbook principles, meant to sit metaphorically on your lap as you navigate the turbulence of real organizational work.

Whether you're walking into a stakeholder meeting, debriefing an incident, or writing a pitch for executive buy-in, this is your last look before wheels-up.

The Security Kneeboard

1. Translate, Don't Transmit

Turn security talk into business talk.

→ Ask: "How would they explain this to their boss?"

2. Story First, Evidence Second

Frame risk as a story with stakes.

→ Ask: "What's the human version of this scenario?"

3. Speak Their Metrics, Not Your Acronyms

Use KPIs they already care about.

→ Ask: "How does this affect revenue, trust, or speed?"

4. Lead with Curiosity

Start with their goals, not your controls.

→ Ask: "What are you trying to achieve here?"

5. Build Trust Before You Need It

Earn credibility during calm so it holds in crisis.

→ Ask: "Have I shown up consistently for this team?"

6. Make Security Their Idea

Let them help shape the solution.

→ Ask: "How would you solve this if security weren't the blocker?"

7. Frame Risk in Business Terms

Translate vulnerabilities into costs, delays, or lost deals.

→ Ask: "What's the business risk if we ignore this?"

8. Offer Choices, Not Ultimatums

Give safe options, not just safe demands.

→ Ask: "Which version of success do you prefer?"

9. Use Empathy as a Strategy, Not a Sentiment

Understand their constraints before proposing yours.

→ Ask: "What pressure are they under right now?"

10. Replace Blame with Inquiry

Treat mistakes as data, not defects.

→ Ask: "What made this choice reasonable at the time?"

11. Practice Psychological Safety

Make it safe to tell you the truth.

→ Ask: "Have I made it okay to say 'I don't know'?"

12. Design for Human Behavior, Not Ideal Policy

Secure the messy real world, not the theoretical one.

→ Ask: "Where are people likely to work around this?"

13. Align Security with Velocity

Secure things early so speed is safer, not slower.

→ Ask: "How can we help you move faster without risk?"

14. Build Security In, Don't Bolt It On

Be part of the design, not just review.

→ Ask: "Can we join the next whiteboard session?"

15. Communicate Readiness, Not Just Maturity

Focus on what's actionable, not just what's documented.

→ Ask: "Can we show how quickly we respond, not just how many controls we've deployed?"

SECURITY INFLUENCE CANVAS

Communication	Relationship Building	Decision Influence	Team Culture & Leadership	Operational Execution
1. Translate, Don't Transmit Ask: "How would they explain this to their boss?"	**4. Lead with Curiosity** Ask: "What are you trying to achieve here?"	**7. Frame Risk in Business Terms** Ask: "What's the business risk if we ignore this?"	**10. Replace Blame with Inquiry** Ask: "What made this choice reasonable at the time?"	**13. Align Security with Velocity** Ask: "How can we help you move faster without risk?"
2. Story First, Evidence Second Ask: "What's the human version of this scenario?"	**5. Build Trust Before You Need It** Ask: "Have I shown up consistently for this team?"	**8. Offer Choices, Not Ultimatums** Ask: "Which version do you prefer?"	**11. Practice Psychological Safety** Ask: "Have I made it okay to say 'I don't know'?"	**14. Build Security In, Don't Bolt It On** Ask: "Can we join the next white-board session?"
3. Speak Their Metrics, Not Your Acronyms Ask: "How does this affect revenue, trust, or speed?"	**6. Make Security Their Idea** Ask: "How would you solve this if security weren't the blocker?"	**9. Use Empathy as a Strategy, Not a Sentiment** Ask: "What pressure are they under right now?"	**12. Design for Human Behavior Not Ideal Policy** Ask: "Where are people likely to work around this?"	**15. Communicate Readiness, Not Just Maturity** Ask: "Can we show how quickly we respond—not just how many controls we've deployed?"

Trifold Rules for Influence Under Pressure

The ATC Rules of Security Influence

- **Acknowledge their priorities.**
  If you can't name what matters to them, you won't influence them.

- **Translate risk into results.**
  If it doesn't affect business outcomes, it won't get airtime.

- **Collaborate, don't command.**
  Influence is built through inclusion, not imposition.

- **Default to empathy.**
  If you're not curious, you're probably wrong.

- **Be brief, be relevant, be real.**
  You don't need to be impressive. You need to be understood.

SECURITY INFLUENCE QUICK REFERENCE

ACKNOWLEDGE THEIR PRIORITIES
If you can't name what matters to them, you won't influence them.

TRANSLATE RISK INTO RESULTS
If it doesn't affect business outcomes, it won't get airtime.

COLLABORATE, DON'T COMMAND
Influence is built through inclusion, not imposition.

DEFAULT TO EMPATHY
If you're not curious, you're probably wrong.

BE BRIEF, BE RELEVANT, BE REAL
You don't need to be impressive. You need to be understood.

About the Author

Joshua C. Mason is a cybersecurity leader, educator, and advocate dedicated to making cybersecurity accessible and integral to business success. With a foundation as a U.S. Air Force cyber warfare officer and pilot, Joshua has transitioned into roles that bridge the gap between technical expertise and strategic business objectives. Oh, he was also a C-130 pilot. Can't believe we made it this far without saying that.

Throughout his career, Joshua has held pivotal positions in both the public and private sectors, including serving as a senior instructor at the Defense Cyber Crime Center's Cyber Training Academy and contributing to the development of the eLearnSecurity Junior Penetration Tester (eJPTv2) certification. His experience spans from hands-on penetration testing to high-level consulting, always emphasizing the alignment of cybersecurity initiatives with overarching business goals.

Beyond his professional roles, Joshua is deeply committed to community building and mentorship. He founded initiatives such as Cyber Supply Drop and Noob Village, aiming to support newcomers to the cybersecurity field, particularly veterans transitioning from military service. As the host of the "Simply Defensive" podcast, he engages with experts to discuss real-world cybersecurity challenges and solutions.

Joshua's approach is characterized by a blend of technical acumen and a passion for teaching. He believes in the power of storytelling and practical guidance to demystify cybersecurity concepts, making them relatable and actionable for professionals across various industries.

www.ingramcontent.com/pod-product-compliance
Lightning Source LLC
Chambersburg PA
CBHW071203210326
41597CB00016B/1658